Teach Yourself®

Understand Greek Civilization

John Purkis

Hodder Education

338 Euston Road, London NW1 3BH.

Hodder Education is an Hachette UK company

First published in UK 1999 by Hodder Education

First published in US 1999 by NTC/Contemporary Publishing,
4255 West Touhy Avenue, Lincolnwood (Chicago), Illinois 60646
1975 USA.

This edition published in UK 2012 by Hodder Education

This edition published in US 2012 by McGraw Hill Companies, Inc.

Hachette UK's policy is to use papers that are natural, renewable
and recyclable products and made from wood grown in sustainable
forests. The logging and manufacturing processes are expected to
conform to the environmental regulations of the country of origin.

www.hoddereducation.co.uk

Typeset by Cenveo Publisher Services.

Front cover: © Anatoly Vartanov – Fotolia

Printed in Great Britain by CPI Group (UK) Ltd, Croydon, CR0 4YY.

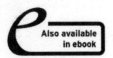

Also available
in ebook

Contents

Meet the author

I joined the Open University when it began and took part in the planning and writing of the courses on *The Greeks* and *Homer*. Later on I taught students on these courses, and was impressed by the enthusiasm with which they pursued their interests. Whatever else is going on in Greece people should remember our debt to the Ancient Greeks and their power to drive things forward. The Greeks founded Western civilization; their literature and architecture provided models for later cultures. They began to think in ways that led to the development of science and philosophy.

Classical studies, which had been reserved for the few until the middle of the last century, have now become available to everybody because of new translations, theatre productions and films, and the growth of tourism. There is a noticeable revival of interest in teaching the Classics in schools, and in many universities Greek may be studied from the beginning. This book is intended to build upon these changes in attitude, and I hope it will introduce you to Greek civilization in the broadest sense. Enjoy.

In one minute

I should like you to think for the moment about what you already know about Greece. Either from books or television, from holidays or from a simple visit to a supermarket, you will find that there are clues that help you to place the Ancient Greek civilization in space and time.

Taking a chronological approach will enable us to survey the various phases of that civilization, beginning with the Bronze Age people known as the Mycenaeans, who seem to have been remembered in the heroic world of Homer. Then we shall visit Olympia, the original site of the Games, and the oracle of Apollo at Delphi. In studying the fifth century BCE, generally reckoned as the height of the Greek achievement, you need to understand the different approaches of the Spartans and the Athenians to managing a city-state; both made different contributions to overcoming the Persians. They collected other cities round them in military alliances, and eventually the two groups entered upon a long war, which ended in the defeat of Athens. Even so, the Athenians embellished their city with splendid architecture, and in their theatre the greatest Greek tragedies were performed. Socrates lived in this period, and his philosophy was presented in the dialogues of Plato.

At the end of the next century the Macedonians, led by Alexander the Great, took over the leadership of Greece. They conquered the Persians and spread Greek language and ideas through much of the known world. New cities were founded and the Library at Alexandria became the centre of Hellenistic culture.

Finally, we consider the transmission of Greek culture down to our own times. After the Roman emperor Constantine had transferred the capital from Rome to Constantinople (now Istanbul) the Eastern half of his empire became the Byzantine Empire, where the preferred language was Greek. Scholars kept the important Greek texts in being and gave them to the West after the fall of Constantinople in 1453 CE.

Introduction

What is the secret of the continuing interest in Greek civilization?
One reason is that for many years the Classical world and its
ideas dominated Western education. Knowledge of the Classical
languages, and in particular of the literary texts in those languages,
was a passport to ruling-class professions. Originally the Greeks
were studied because they were regarded as a high point of human
achievement; when they were rediscovered in the Renaissance this
amounted to a rediscovery of civilization. That is, they defined
what the word civilization meant. This attitude has descended from
the Renaissance through the education system almost down to the
present day. In the nineteenth century, grammar and public school
education for boys largely consisted of compulsory Greek and Latin.
Things have now changed, and pessimists will point to the number of
students studying the ancient language in schools as being in decline,
though it must be pointed out that there is no longer the compulsory
element in this.

It is good that that kind of pressure has gone. Nowadays there
is a general revival of interest in the Classical world; pupils are
choosing to study this area because they want to. This is matched
by a continuing upsurge of interest among adults in 'Classics in
Translation' or general courses about the background to the Classics.

People will accuse me of confusing Greek studies with 'the Classics',
and I have no particular wish to set Greeks above Romans, or to
enter into a debate about the relative worth of the two Classical areas
of study. Because of the increase in knowledge we can now see that
the Mediterranean world from 2000 BCE to 1453 CE, which is an
enormous part of world history, presents many more opportunities
than the old 'classic periods' ever did, and I have tried to indicate this
in this book.

The enduring appeal of the Greeks and their civilization remains with
us and seems to be just as firmly based as it always was. The Greeks

have won a reputation for inventiveness and imagination which continues to fascinate students; it also intrigues those who take a holiday in Greece and want to understand the unexpected treasures which they find in the cities and museums. In writing this book I have tried to keep in mind people who have come to this area of study for the first time or who have been thrilled with enthusiasm by what they have seen on holiday. In the arrangement of material I have tried to link the ideas to archaeological and other sites which are frequently seen in tours of Greece today. It would be impossible to provide a complete picture of Greek history, literature or art in a book of this kind. An account of a civilization can be broken down into a series of cultural phases and each one of those has been identified with a well-known site or city. These are linked by an outline historical narrative, and references to the people who lived in the city may provide a jumping-off point for an exploration of an intellectual or artistic theme; in this way religion, philosophy and other associated topics are introduced. From time to time extracts from Greek literature are incorporated to give an opportunity for students to listen to the voices of Ancient Greece.

Dates

The dating system used in this book may not be familiar to you. In Classical studies it is now quite common to substitute the abbreviations BCE (Before Common Era) for BC and CE (Common Era) for AD. The most important century in Greek history was probably the fifth century (i.e. the century beginning with the year 500 and therefore with dates falling between the years 499–401 BCE); the next century is called the fourth century, with the dates in the 300s. Even when this has become familiar it still involves you in backward reckoning which can cause confusion at first, especially when you are used to dates which are counted forwards.

Translations

In this book nearly all the translated passages are taken from the Penguin Classics series. This will make it easier for the student to find the complete texts in a bookshop, online or a public library, and the references and bibliography in these texts should be useful starting points for further study.

Transliteration

In transcribing names into English the Greek letters are not always represented by their exact equivalents in English. The reason for this is that our received names of the Greeks have been modified by the transmission through Latin. This is why the traditional English forms are under attack at present. Should we say Attika or Attica? Generally speaking I have preferred to keep to the standard English transliteration of Greek names, although one must be aware that many books now use Herodotos for Herodotus (easy?) or Aiskhulos for Aeschylus (too hard?); I have, therefore, kept to the standard English pronunciation of these names as well, and used it when introducing them to the reader.

Acknowledgements

In preparing this book I am grateful for help and encouragement received from Open University colleagues, in particular Paula James and Chris Wilson, although they are not, of course, responsible for the way the book has come out. I should like to thank my wife, Sallie Purkis, for restructuring the entire manuscript in a drastic and helpful way.

1

Orientation: Locating the Greeks in space and time

Aim

The aim of this chapter is to point you in the direction of Ancient Greece. At the end of the chapter you should be able to give outline answers to the following questions:

▶ Who were the Ancient Greeks? (We'll call them 'the Greeks' from now on, and if we are speaking of Modern Greeks the context will make this clear.)

▶ When did Greek civilization take place? (What are the historical parameters? When did the period which we call 'Classical' occur, and what preceded and succeeded it?)

▶ Where did the Greeks live?

▶ How do we know about them?

▶ Why are Greek pottery and vase-painting so important to us?

Below are the important Greek names encountered in this chapter with a note on their *English* pronunciation.

ZEUS (*Zioos* – one syllable). Chief Greek god. Father of gods and men.

HERA (*Here-a*). Chief Greek goddess, consort of Zeus.

AESCHYLUS (*Ee-skill-us*; stress on the first syllable). First important Classical playwright.

HERODOTUS (say as written with stress on second syllable). First historian and prose writer.

XERXES (*zerk-zees*) Ruler of Persia.

AGAMEMNON (stress on third syllable). Ruler of Mycenae; legendary commander of Greek forces at Troy.

ARISTOTLE (stress on third syllable). Fourth-century philosopher.

Your Greek holiday – first impressions of 'Greekness'

A VISIT TO GREECE

It seems best to begin from the present situation and from what we
know. Many of you will have been to Greece on holiday, or could
go if you wished to do so. This may well be the reason that led you
to read this book. This ease of access to Greece is a relatively recent
phenomenon and actually gives you a tremendous advantage over
earlier students. There was a time, say 200 years ago, when the Greek
language – I mean, of course, the language in which the ancient texts
were written – was studied by only comparatively few middle- or
upper-class young men in Western European countries, but until
the end of the nineteenth century hardly any of these would have
had the opportunity to visit Greece itself, however rich they might
have been. During the First World War, for quite different reasons,
a much larger group of young men, as soldiers, were forced to make
the acquaintance of Thessalonika, or visited Greek islands on their
way to Gallipoli; this experience of campaigning in Greece was also
available for a short period during and after the Second World War.
It is only since the 1960s that a Greek holiday has become cheap
enough for many people to enjoy.

Of course, a holiday need not be combined with study, but since
the growth and popularization of archaeology some of the sites that
archaeologists and historians have worked on have become accessible
to tourists, and therefore to students like yourself. Even if you are
not able to visit the country, it is possible to get a good idea of Greek
scenery, and the archaeological sites, thanks to the extraordinary
light and the clear air of Greece. Photographic images of the country
surround us in the form of posters, television programmes or book
illustrations.

PRESENT-DAY EXAMPLES OF GREEK EMIGRATION AND TRADE

The Greeks travel too. Today you will meet Greeks in London,
Greeks in America, Greeks in Australia. On my first trip from Athens
to Sparta I was introduced to a fellow passenger on the bus; he had
been living in Australia for more than 40 years and had come back
to retire to the family house which his sister had looked after all
that time. He returned with all his possessions in a 1930s suitcase,
probably the one he had set out with. In fact, his spoken English was
minimal, as he had worked on a Greek-speaking farm, far away from

any Australian city. He had not been able to see much of Australia as he had sent most of his wages home to Greece.

What general points might you pick up from this anecdote?
(Just make the obvious comments; there is no hidden mystery.)

Answer

▶ The land in Greece cannot support all its inhabitants.
▶ Greeks will travel anywhere and work hard to earn a living.
▶ Greeks are attached to home.
▶ Greeks, possibly, prefer to speak Greek.

These points are, in fact, of some general application, even though they derive from an anecdote, and the general points may help us to understand the people of Ancient Greece, too. (See 'Where did the Greeks live?' later in this chapter.)

What products of modern Greece can you find in your local supermarket?

Answer

Olives, olive oil, currants, raisins, figs, yoghurt, honey and – particularly if there is a local group of Greeks – Greek sweets and wine.

Discussion

In fact, the Greeks have always traded widely with versions of these products. At some of the earliest sites in Greece, such as Pylos (a Mycenaean 'palace', dated to the thirteenth century BCE, which we shall visit in Chapter 2), copious facilities for storing oil and wine have been found. At that period the oil was prepared with different kinds of scents and flavours. We have little idea what ancient wine tasted like as various preservatives were added.

Insight

In the fifth century BCE Hermippus described Athenian imports as follows:

From Cyrene silphium [asafoetida] and ox hides, from the Hellespont mackerel and all kinds of salted fish, from Italy salt and ribs of beef ... from Egypt sails and rope, from Syria frankincense, from Crete cypress for the gods; Libya provides abundant ivory to buy, Rhodes raisins and sweet figs, but from Euboea pears and fat apples. Slaves from Phrygia, ...Pagasae provides tattooed slaves, Paphlagonia dates and oily almonds, Phoenicia dates and fine wheat-flour, Carthage rugs and many-coloured cushions.

Russell Meiggs, *The Athenian Empire* p. 264

But you may well say, looking at this range of products, that there is not really enough here to generate much wealth, then or now.

How then have recent Greek millionaires, such as Aristotle Onassis, amassed so much money?

Answer

The point is that the Greeks are professional traders, acting as third parties in the trade between other countries, taking oil from the Middle East to all parts of the world in their tankers.

Discussion

It is quite possible to imagine small-scale versions of this in the Ancient World. Such trading depends on bargaining, on quick thinking and fast talking. These all contribute to our image of 'Greekness'; some of you will have memories of holidays in Greece which will help you to appreciate this – you may remember the Greeks as always talking, always asking questions and always, if necessary, ready with the answers.

'GREEKNESS': AN EXAMPLE FROM HERODOTUS

Let us now pursue this aspect of 'Greekness' further by looking at a passage written by Herodotus, who lived approximately between 490 BCE and 420 BCE. You may have heard of him as the unacknowledged 'star' of the film *The English Patient*. We shall meet him later, as the historian of the Persian Wars. In his book *The Histories* he cannot resist asking questions about everything wherever he goes, whether or not it has anything to do with the Persian Wars. Here he is in Egypt trying to understand the annual flooding of the Nile.

> *About why the Nile behaves precisely as it does I could get no information from the priests or anyone else. What I particularly wished to know was why the water begins to rise at the summer solstice, continues to do so for a hundred days, and then falls again at the end of that period, so that it remains low throughout the winter until the summer solstice comes round again in the following year. Nobody in Egypt could give me any explanation of this, in spite of my constant attempts to find out what was the peculiar property which made the Nile behave in the opposite way to other rivers, and why – another point on which I hoped for information – it was the only river to cause no breezes.*

Certain Greeks, hoping to advertise how clever they are, have tried to account for the flooding of the Nile in three different ways. Two of the explanations are not worth dwelling upon, beyond a bare mention of what they are: one is that the summer north winds cause the water to rise by checking the flow of the current towards the sea. In fact, however, these winds on many occasions have failed to blow, yet the Nile has risen as usual; moreover, if these winds were responsible for the rise, the other rivers which happen to run against them would certainly be affected in the same way as the Nile – and to a greater extent, in that they are smaller and have a less powerful current. There are many such rivers in Syria and Libya, but none of them are affected in the same way as the Nile. The second explanation is less rational, being somewhat, if I may so put it, of a legendary character: it is that the Nile exhibits its remarkable characteristics because it flows from the Ocean, the stream of which encircles the world. The third theory is much the most plausible, but at the same time furthest from the truth; according to this, the water of the Nile comes from melting snow, but as it flows from Libya through Ethiopia into Egypt, that is, from a very hot into a cooler climate, how could it possibly originate in snow? Obviously, this view is as worthless as the other two. Anyone who can use his wits about such matters will find plenty of arguments to prove how unlikely it is that snow is the cause of the flooding of the river: the strongest proof is provided by the winds, which blow hot from those regions; secondly rain and frost are unknown there – and after snow rain is bound to fall within five days. So that if there were snow in that part of the world, there would necessarily be rain too; thirdly, the natives are black because of the hot climate. Again, hawks and swallows remain throughout the year, and cranes migrate thither in winter to escape the cold weather of Scythia. But if there were any snow, however little, in the region through which the Nile flows and in which it rises, none of these things could possibly be; for they are contrary to reason. As to the writer who mentions the Ocean in this connexion, his account is a mere fairy-tale depending upon an unknown quantity and cannot therefore be disproved by argument. I know myself of no river called Ocean, and can only suppose that Homer or some earlier poet invited the name and introduced it into poetry. If, after criticizing these theories, I must express an opinion myself about

**a matter so obscure as the reason why the Nile floods in summer,
I would say (to put the whole thing in the fewest words) that
during winter the sun is driven out of his course by storms towards
the upper parts of Libya. It stands to reason that the country
nearest to, and most directly under, the sun should be most
short of water, and that the streams which feed the rivers in that
neighbourhood should most readily dry up.**

Herodotus, The Histories, Book 2

*What do you make of this? Please note down anything that occurs
to you.*

Discussion

The first paragraph makes it clear that the Egyptians have no
explanation to offer for the flooding of the Nile. One reason for their
indifference might be that they know only about the Nile and so
cannot make comparisons with other rivers. The thing that baffles
Herodotus is that no one, not even the priests, who are supposed to be
the intellectuals, has ever asked the question. Putting it another way,
the Egyptian 'mindset', which seems to have relied on a mythological
depiction of the universe, was incapable of seeing the need to ask
speculative questions. (By 'mythological' here I mean that explanations
were offered in stories which encapsulated a religious or semi-religious
truth.) This way of thinking and the Greek challenge to it will be fully
discussed in Chapters 3 and 4, but even as you read this section of
Herodotus, you should begin to see why the Greeks seem so relevant
to our own scientific outlook, even though the Egyptians were just as
intelligent and had laid the basis of so much of our civilization.

The second paragraph deals with the three explanations given by the
Greeks – notice the irony in the first sentence; perhaps some Greek
advanced thinking is too ingenious. Nevertheless, Herodotus, who
is very fair, gives us the two accounts which he is going to reject.
Surprisingly the third explanation, which *we know* is nearest to the
truth – it is not the snow but the monsoon rains – is also rejected,
and Herodotus ends up with his movable sun hypothesis. (In early
thinking the sun moved rapidly, over, under and round what was
thought to be the flat disc of the earth, every day.)

The 'Greekness' here seems to lie in the openness and quality of
the discussion. Thought has been emancipated from mythological

thinking. Herodotus, incidentally, is believed to have been the first Greek prose writer and the ease and unaffected nature of his style charms us into agreement.

Who were the Greeks?

In answering this question we need to split it into two and deal first with problems of origins and second with what we would now call national identity.

ORIGINS

We have to think what is involved here. Are we looking for a group of people who resemble each other in some way or are we looking for speakers of the Greek language? This second alternative seems a more fruitful line of enquiry, and we can begin with the fact that linguistics experts classify Greek as an Indo-European language, related to both Sanskrit and Latin.

The Indo-European hypothesis

Until recently, scholars believed that there had been an invasion of Indo-European speakers from the area north of Greece, who had brought the Greek language with them. (You can read more about this theory and the arguments against it in a book by Colin Renfrew called: *Archaeology and Language: The Puzzle of Indo-European Origins* – see Chapter 10). This invasion was thought to be paralleled by religious developments, in which the male sky god Zeus was supposed to have encountered powerful female goddesses already established in Greece, for example, Hera at Argos: the diplomatic marriages, relationships and liaisons between Zeus and these resident goddesses were thought to explain the amorous chaos of Greek mythology.

Recent abandonment of this hypothesis

The difficulty is that there is no written history or other evidence to indicate whether this Indo-European invasion ever happened. Generally speaking, the old way of explaining cultural or linguistic change by a series of 'invasions' is no longer thought to be necessary or desirable. A more modern view is that most people – and their descendants, of course – have always lived in the same place, and that there are many internal reasons why language and culture change. If you think of an example from recent times, the reason that English is widely spoken on the Indian sub-continent may be the result of an 'invasion' in the first instance, but we know that the population of India remained in place. Now that the 'invaders' have gone, why is the language still generally used many years after they have departed?

Legends relating to the first Greeks

The Greeks themselves had various legends about their origins – Europa and the bull, Cadmus's arrival at Thebes, the daughters of Danaos at Argos – which indicated origins in the Eastern Mediterranean, Phoenicia or Egypt. And in the legend of the Minotaur, Athens had, at one time, paid tribute to Crete.

The legend of Theseus and the Minotaur

In legendary times Minos was the King of Crete; his wife Pasiphae was enamoured of a bull and the resulting offspring – the Minotaur – was hidden in the recesses of the Royal palace, in a series of winding passages called the Labyrinth. Minos demanded regular tribute from Athens in the form of seven young men and seven young women, who were placed in the Labyrinth and eaten by the Minotaur.

Theseus was the son of the King of Athens; he insisted on accompanying the ship taking the tribute and was determined to kill the Minotaur. He was assisted by the daughter of Minos, the Princess Ariadne, who gave him a ball of thread so that he could find his way back afterwards. He left for home with Ariadne but abandoned her on Naxos.

Like all mythological stories there are many strange features, but the detail of the tribute being paid from Athens to Crete has support in other accounts of Minos and his supremacy over the Aegean at that time (hence the term 'Minoan' civilization).

Different linguistic groupings

The fifth-century Greeks had no clear knowledge of their origins apart from these legends, but they could recognize the presence of different dialects of the Greek language. They referred to these as Attic, Ionic and Doric and were quite clear about how these dialects had come about. They said that certain areas like Attica – the district where Athens is situated and where the inhabitants spoke the Attic dialect of Greek – and Arcadia, in the centre of the Peloponnese, contained an indigenous population, perhaps related to an early and half-forgotten people called the Pelasgians, who were thought to

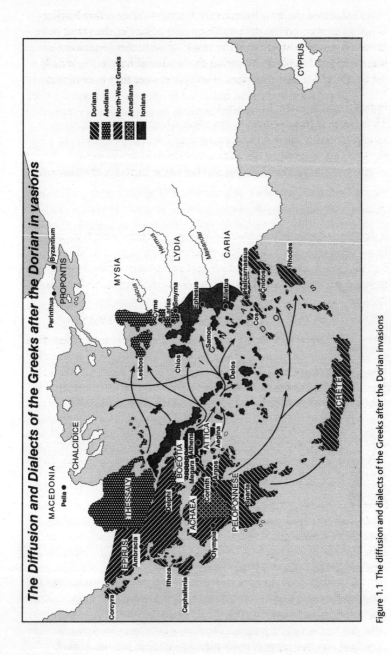

Figure 1.1 The diffusion and dialects of the Greeks after the Dorian invasions

have inhabited the whole peninsula and the islands in former times. They also preserved an oral tradition of the Dorian invasions, circa 1000 BCE, which had placed the Spartans and other groups in their current positions; 'Dorian' means those who spoke the Doric dialect of Greek. (Once again modern scholarship would play down the size of population movement indicated by the word 'invasion'.) The displacement of the previous inhabitants by the Dorians explained the presence of the Ionians in what had, therefore, become known as Ionia (on the western fringe of present-day Turkey – see Figure 1.1).

DID THE GREEKS REGARD THEMSELVES AS A SINGLE NATIONAL UNIT?

In answering this question you must first of all obliterate present-day ideas from your mind; there was no sense of what we would call 'nationalism'. Although the Greeks in Classical times were disunited, owing allegiance only to their local city (see below), they still believed that *collectively* they were the Hellenes. From the traditional date of 776 BCE the Greek cities had all met at Olympia in the Peloponnese, a site dedicated to Zeus, for the Olympic Games (see Chapter 3). Similarly the religious centres at Dodona, an oracle sacred to Zeus, and at Delphi, the seat of Apollo's oracle, were regarded as common to all Greeks.

> **Insight**
> 'Hellenes' was the regular name used by the Greeks about their own people. Note that the word 'Greeks' is what the Romans called them.

The identity of the Greek people was regularly affirmed by attendance at these religious centres and their associated ceremonies – and by mutual help at moments of crisis. Although there was no organized nationhood beyond this, they were able to define themselves in relation to the other groups, who were clearly foreigners, such as the peoples of Asia.

> **Insight**
> 'Barbarians' was the name given to foreigners; i.e. those whose speech sounded like 'bar bar'. It is important to understand that at first there was no anti-foreigner prejudice in this word.

Unity in the face of an external threat

If you thought that the various stories of origins were rather like the English claiming to derive from the Angles, Saxons and Jutes, this next section is to be compared with the fact that the one piece of history that the English never forget is the story of the Spanish Armada. England was in danger of extinction as a nation; but the Armada was defeated – 'God blew and they were scattered'. At the beginning of the fifth century the Greeks were threatened by the supreme enemy – Persia – and somehow survived (see Chapters 4, 5 and 6). As time went on the Greeks repeatedly told themselves this story and extrapolated a kind of national glory from it; they thought they were clearly superior, though not in military strength, for they knew that Persia could put literally millions of troops into the field. What the Greeks had was an inquisitive kind of intelligence, that would not let problems remain unsolved, and self-control which was a compound of good taste, common sense and keeping cool in a crisis: the proverbial 'moderation in all things'. Barbarians, on the other hand, tended to be perceived as showy, ill-disciplined and ignorant: in particular, they were sure to go 'over the top' where a project or building or poetic style was in question. A famous example of this was the occasion when Xerxes, the Persian king, punished the Hellespont (the Dardanelles).

He then prepared to move forward to Abydos, where a bridge had already been constructed across the Hellespont from Asia to Europe. Between Sestos and Madytus in the Chersonese there is a rocky headland running out into the water opposite Abydos. This headland was the point to which Xerxes' engineers carried their two bridges from Abydos – a distance of seven furlongs. One was constructed by the Phoenicians using flax cables, the other by the Egyptians with papyrus cables. The work was successfully completed, but a subsequent storm of great violence smashed it up and carried everything away. Xerxes was very angry when he learned of the disaster, and gave orders that the Hellespont should receive three hundred lashes and have a pair of fetters thrown into it. I have heard before now that he also sent people to brand it with hot irons. He certainly instructed the men with the whips to utter, as they wielded them, the barbarous and presumptuous words: 'You salt and bitter stream, your master lays this punishment upon you for injuring him, who never injured you. But Xerxes the King will cross you, with or without your permission. No man sacrifices to you, and you deserve the neglect by your acid and muddy waters.' In addition to punishing the Hellespont Xerxes gave orders that the men responsible for building the bridges should have their heads cut off. The men who received these invidious orders duly carried them out, and other engineers completed the work.

Herodotus, *The Histories*, Book 7

Insight

As Edward Said has shown us in his book *Orientalism* (see the booklist in Chapter 10), there is a negative side to all this. Because of the almost unconscious absorption of such attitudes towards the barbarians, the British, French and other Europeans, as heirs to the Greeks, had little or no respect for the civilizations which they in turn encountered in Asia, and 'Oriental' became a term which signified 'how different from us'.

If they were not a nation, how then did the Greeks organize themselves politically?

THE CITY-STATE

It is disconcerting for us to find that the primary political unit was the city and that this was regarded as the ideal. This division of Greece into small units was largely determined by geography, for example, the many small islands, and the lack of land transport. The mountains interpose themselves between the different cities, so that even today it seems amazing that the bus is able to climb from Argos on to the plateau of the Peloponnese. As you read the histories of the fifth century you notice that the armies move about slowly on foot; the navies on the other hand move rapidly from place to place.

The cities differed one from the other because of their political organization. We shall need to define some terms.

What is the meaning of the following terms?

▶ Kingship
▶ Oligarchy
▶ Tyranny
▶ Democracy

If you can, explain how they might apply to the Greeks.

Answer and discussion

▶ *Kingship*, the word to us and to the Greeks really means a good or acceptable version of monarch. The Classical Greeks thought of kingship as something that had existed in the remote past. In Homer, Agamemnon was a great king, but this was in a fairytale world. It is true that, in historical times, many cities, including Athens, had an official called 'king' as part of the constitution, but he fulfilled ceremonial and religious functions. In the fifth century some barbarian empires were ruled by kings on a larger scale, for example, the Great King of Persia and the Pharaoh of Egypt, but you could argue that these societies were survivors from the Bronze Age. Nearer home, powerful kings operated in Macedonia, which was thought of as being on the fringes of the Greek world. Kingship was reintroduced into Greece by Alexander the Great, who came from Macedonia. It became the norm in the Hellenistic period.

▶ *Oligarchy* means 'government by the few'. There might be an oligarchy of powerful traders or rich men, but after a time it would become rule 'by the best families', and therefore 'by an aristocracy'. Such governments hated democracy, because it allowed the lower classes into power. Although this may seem odd to us, it was a common form of rule in Greece.

▶ *Tyranny*, which means despotic or arbitrary rule to us, simply means 'rule by one person' here and does not necessarily have the connotations of the English word. Tyrannies could be established by violence and, thereafter, were inherited within families, or could be simply seized as opportunity allowed. It was not the same as kingship, however, and was more like the rule of a dictator.

▶ *Democracy* means 'government by the people', which we operate using elections and control by the various literate means which we call public opinion. To the Greeks it also implied 'by the many' (in contrast to the 'few' in the definition of oligarchy) and this conveyed class implications. Democracy was often established by violence i.e. the expulsion of a tyrant or 'the few'. Because of the small size of Greek cities it was, in theory, possible for all the citizens to assemble in the marketplace to make decisions and to express public opinion by shouting: but in practice people were elected to carry out governmental functions.

Were these systems unchangeable?

Answer

Aristotle, a philosopher who wrote in the fourth century, tried to analyse Greek political systems. His view was that states passed from kingship to oligarchy or aristocratic rule; then there would come a coup or sudden switch to tyranny as one man or family defeated the other aristocrats. This was not such a bad thing as it seemed, because it prepared the way for a transition to democracy. One of the hidden elements of bias behind Herodotus's hatred of Xerxes is the fact that Greece had, by and large, passed through an age of tyrants in the sixth century BCE, and in his time (the fifth century BCE) was divided into free cities which embraced democracy or oligarchy.

How did Greek democracy differ from ours?

Answer

Though these political systems caused intense debate in Greece at the time it is not so easy for us to get excited as we have become used to regarding democracy as the norm; on the other hand, we have not experienced a true tyranny in Britain since the time of Charles I, who ruled without Parliament for ten years. There is considerable controversy about the nature of Greek democracy, with some saying that it is the ancestor of the present constitutional arrangements of Western Europe and America; while others say that we should not be able to recognize it as having any resemblance at all. Indeed, there have been so many versions of democracy in the twentieth century – including 'people's republics' and 'guided democracy' – that we may want to idealize the Greek model.

It is, therefore, unsettling to discover that even in Athens, where the adult male population formed the democracy, foreigners and slaves made up so much of the population that they outnumbered the citizens; of course, these subordinate classes did not have a vote. Nor did women, who were largely confined to the home and to household duties, and there has been much debate about their influence on public affairs. On the one hand there is evidence of a real lack of freedom; on the other hand, the drama shows women taking leading roles in the stories, although all the actors were male.

CONCLUSION

Although not all Greeks were citizens of a democracy, they were generally suspicious of barbarian kings and the 'master–slave' politics which an unchecked monarchy encouraged. They had, therefore, a keen sense of the un-Greek behaviour in which such rulers indulged, and which usually led to excess and, possibly, provoked the anger of the gods. Democracy, on the other hand, meant that you had to learn to persuade people to agree with you and to act.

Below is a famous example of this from Xenophon's *Anabasis*, or *The Persian Expedition*. In the year 401 BCE Xenophon, who was a Greek general, was involved in leading home a Greek mercenary army that found itself isolated on the banks of a river in the heart of the Persian Empire; through a treacherous manoeuvre the Persians had captured most of their generals. It was assumed that, leaderless, they would collapse into chaos – as would have been the case with barbarians. In practice, they form an assembly to make decisions – a sort of Greek democratic city in motion – and are persuaded by Xenophon not to give in but to march for home. (The 'King' is the King of Persia.) This is part of Xenophon's speech:

> *Now, personally, while the truce was in force, I could never stop feeling sorry for us and looking with envy on the King and those on his side. I considered what a large and splendid country they had, what inexhaustible supplies, what quantities of servants, of cattle and gold and clothing material; and then I thought on the other hand of our men's prospects – that we could only get a share of all these good things by paying for it (and I knew that there were not many left who had the money to do so), and that the oaths we had sworn prevented us from acquiring supplies in any other way except by paying for them. When I reckoned all this up, I sometimes used to feel more misgivings about the truce than I now do about the war. Now, however, they have put an end to the truce, and I think that the period of their arrogance and of our uneasy feelings is also ended. For now these good things lie in front of us as prizes for whichever side shows itself to be the better men; the gods are judges of the contest, and they will naturally be on our side, since it was our enemies who took their names in vain, while we, with many good things before our eyes, resolutely kept our hands off them because of the oaths we had sworn to the gods. So it seems to me that we can enter the contest with much more confidence than they can. Then we are physically better able than they are to endure cold and heat and hardship; our morale is, with the gods on our side, better than theirs; and if the gods grant us victory, as they did before, our enemies are easier to wound and kill than we are. Quite likely there are others who feel the same as I do. Well then, in heaven's name, let us not wait for other people to come to us and call upon us to do great deeds.*

With such self-confidence, the Greeks thought they could take on the world.

When were the Greeks?

Date BCE			
	c. 2500	Cycladic civilization	NEOLITHIC
	1900–1600	Minoan civilization based in Crete	BRONZE
	1600–1200	Mycenaean period	AGE
	c. 1000	Dark Ages	IRON AGE
	700–500	Archaic period	
	500–323	Classical age	
	323–50	Hellenistic age	
	50 BCE–400 CE	Roman Empire	
	400–1453	Byzantine Empire	
	1453–1820	Turkish domination	
	1820–present	Emergence of modern Greece as a nation-state	

We need to begin by defining some of the standard chronological terms. The table above is provided simply to enable you to identify the main periods of Greek history, and quite soon you will learn to recognize these terms and what they refer to. None of these dates is fixed or exact, except 323 BCE, which refers to the death of Alexander and 1453 CE, which is the date of the fall of Constantinople.

OTHER MEANS OF DATING

We know about the earlier periods only through archaeology, but because of frequent changes in styles of pottery, we can usually place any site we find in a sequential position. Vases can help us to date sites, although we need to allow for the use of a vase before it was buried in the earth; sometimes what appear to be new vases are used in funerals and subsequently placed in a tomb. This may lead archaeologists to give a reasonably exact date.

Insight

Pots are all-important in the study of Greek civilization.

They were the 'plastic' of the age, and they were turned out in enormous quantities by what we may describe as small factories.

They were, in each period, limited to certain basic types, designs, and kinds of decoration.

They were thrown away after use and were also deliberately placed underground to hold the ashes of the dead.

Complete vases or fragments of pots from the earliest times through to the Roman period may be found on all ancient sites in the Mediterranean area and these help us to date what is found in conjunction with them.

DECORATION ON ATHENIAN VASES

It is possible to arrive at a more precise account of the Athenian pottery industry in the Archaic and Classical periods from, say, 600 BCE. The pots were used to export olive oil and wine, and so turn up in central Italy, for example. At some point the potters seem to have become conscious of themselves as artists so that some vases were skilfully decorated; they were treasured by their purchasers or were given as prizes at the games.

The vases produced in the sixth century BCE are usually called black-figure. The clay of Attica turns red when fired and the design was painted on with a solution of black clay; this could be further refined by scratching away the black coating. After about 500 BCE the process was reversed; the whole vase was coated in black, which provided the background to the figures; these were left in the red of the original clay.

The importance of the scenes on vases

The scenes on the vases are frequently of mythological figures, but sometimes we cannot recognize the stories from the accounts in literature. This is evidence of the circulation of oral stories among the people. For example, there is nothing in Homer's poems which could give rise to the scene in Figure 1.2 of Achilles playing a board game in his tent.

In addition, a careful study of the structures surrounding some of the figures reveals that we may be looking at a scene from a theatrical presentation of the story. Other vases show scenes of everyday activities, for example, an olive tree being beaten; these are exceptionally precious as we do not have much pictorial or other evidence of social life.

THE TRADITIONAL FOCUS ON THE CLASSICAL AGE

When we enter the truly historical period – after, say, 500 BCE – we have documents and monuments to help us, which can often be dated exactly. Traditionally, Greek studies have always been focussed on the Classical period, which is when most of the important authors

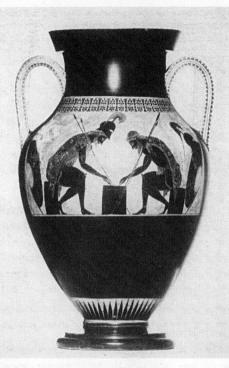

Figure 1.2 Amphora with Ajax and Achilles playing draughts

flourished and the language and styles of art and architecture were believed to have reached their highest point.

Architectural features

The history of architecture is a separate subject, but you should familiarize yourself with the three kinds of column (see Figure 1.3). (The names do not match the localities to which they seem to refer and which you will learn about in the next section.) The Parthenon at Athens, which is not a Doric city, has Doric columns. The Ionic is Hellenistic and the Roman Corinthian much later still. The general direction seems to be away from simplicity, but there are exceptions.

Few temples in Greece have survived in anything approaching a complete state, but there is an important example, away from the main cities. On an archaeological tour of Greece you may be taken to

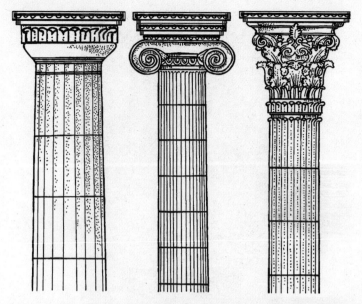

Figure 1.3 Architectural 'orders' shown in design of columns. From left to right: Doric (the Parthenon); Ionic (the Temple of Artemis, Magnesia); and Corinthian (the Temple of Castor, Rome)

the temple of Apollo at Bassae. In a remote part of the Peloponnese a local community erected a splendid building during the second half of the fifth century to honour Apollo, perhaps for his help, or in fulfilment of a special vow undertaken by Arcadian mercenaries at the time of the Peloponnesian War. The sculptured frieze is now in the British Museum.

Insight
'Taste' and All That

This is probably not your first acquaintance with Greek Art and all of us have inherited certain prejudices. Do be cautious about applying out-of-date critical preconceptions to the above examples.

▶ Generally speaking, taste in art has changed considerably since the eighteenth century when the serious study of art history began. The perfectly formed statues which were then in vogue are now regarded as rather boring; indeed, some of the works which thrilled in the eighteenth century (see Figure 8.2) are now thought to be Roman copies or even forgeries.
▶ Archaic statues and even Cycladic figures (see Figure 1.4) were more of an inspiration for the early twentieth century. Of course, far more information about the earlier periods has come to hand and knowledge has increased, so the boundaries of study have been pushed out.

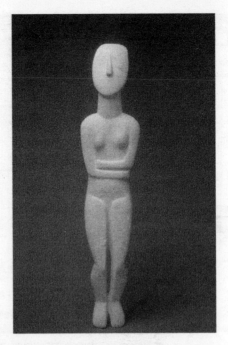

Figure 1.4 Cycladic figure in white marble 2500–2000 BCE

> ▶ On the other hand, it must still be recognized that most of the really
>   interesting artefacts and texts were produced in the Classical period.
> ▶ It is worth remembering that the artists, sculptors and authors themselves
>   did not know which period they were living in, nor that they were 'Archaic'
>   or 'Hellenistic' in their style. Of course, they would know if they were
>   under the domination of a foreign power.

LATER DEVELOPMENTS

▶ In the late fourth century Alexander the Great conquered the
  Persian Empire, and because that empire had controlled large
  areas beyond Persia, he campaigned in what is now Afghanistan
  and Pakistan. These conquests were consolidated by Alexander's
  generals. The Greek-speaking world was now extended to
  include Egypt and Western Asia, and from this time we date the
  beginning of the Hellenistic period.

▶ During the period of the Roman Empire, though political
  control was taken away, the Greek language continued to

grow in influence and was not displaced by Latin in the eastern Mediterranean and Western Asia. This helps to explain why the Gospels were written in Greek.

▶ When Constantine moved the capital of the Roman Empire from Rome to Byzantium (which was then renamed Constantinople), a new Greek-speaking Roman Empire rose, controlling the eastern Mediterranean. Its Christian Church extended Greek influence into Russia. There will be more about Byzantium in Chapter 9.

Where did the Greeks live?

A WORLD WITHOUT FRONTIERS

The rigid boundaries of modern nation-states are misleading. At no time were the Greeks confined to the area we now think of as Greece. Much of the mainland of Greece is mountainous and unsuitable for agriculture. The inhabitants were often forced to live in niches on the coast, though there were some open areas inland, for example, Thessaly. The islands were often more suitable for settlement, but were limited in other ways, needing to be supplied with raw materials from elsewhere; you may know that at the present time some islands have to be supplied with water from tankers, and one has to assume that in the past these islands had similar problems. There was, therefore, a considerable need for more land, or for alternative sources from which to obtain subsistence. This involved setting up trading stations further afield.

COLONIZATION

In fact, the earliest Greeks had dispersed themselves around the known world in Mycenaean times – the prehistoric period before 1000 BCE (see earlier discussed chronology), but many of the settlements discovered by archaeologists on these early sites may have been overwhelmed in the collapse of central power at the end of the Mycenaean period.

A large number of areas of the Mediterranean and Black Sea coastline were occupied in the seventh and sixth centuries BCE, and most of the 'colonies' prospered and remained in place throughout the Classical period.

WHY WERE THESE EARLY COLONISTS SENT OUT?

The reasons for these early emigrations would seem to be as follows:

- ▶ Overpopulation: the poor soil of much of Greece, which had already lost its forest cover and suffered greatly from erosion, could not support the numbers of people who inhabited the successful new cities of the seventh and sixth centuries.
- ▶ The need to secure sources of raw materials and foodstuffs. The Ancient Greeks dispersed themselves in order to extend and protect their trade (see Figure 1.5).

What does Figure 1.5 show us?

Answer

We can see that at one stage the trade of the Mediterranean world was divided between the Greeks and the Phoenicians who were based on Tyre and then on Carthage.

GREEK GEOGRAPHICAL KNOWLEDGE

What knowledge did the Greeks have about the areas beyond their direct political control?

Answer

Not much.

Discussion

Exploration overland was difficult to undertake when there were few roads and no rapid form of land transport. It is worth commenting here on the rather limited extent of Greek geographical knowledge during the Classical period. Although the Greeks had settled the coastline of various land areas, they seem to have had little curiosity about pushing inland, so that in Herodotus's *Histories* (c. 430 BCE) the hinterland of Europe, Asia and Africa remained inhabited by legendary beings. This view of the world had improved little upon the voyage of the Argonauts, which

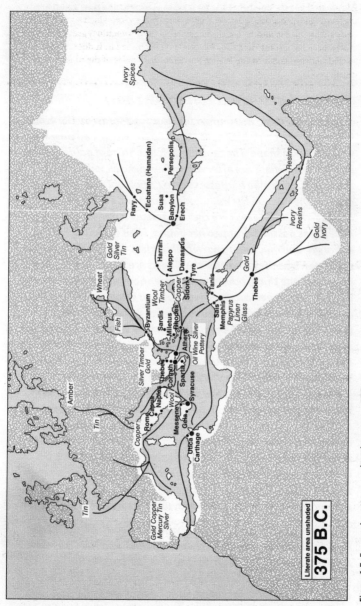

Figure 1.5 Economic patterns and trade routes c. 375 BCE

is a mythical narrative probably based on real exploration of the Black Sea area at an early period. This lack of information is particularly to be noticed when studying Aeschylus' *Prometheus Bound*, for example. Herodotus tries to account for the blank spaces on the map, but gives us what seem to be impossible stories.

Read the following story and comment upon it. A likely story? What do you think of Herodotus as a researcher?

These creatures as they burrow underground throw up the sand in heaps, just as ants in Greece throw up the earth, and they are very similar in shape. The sand has a rich content of gold, and this it is that the Indians are after when they make expeditions into the desert. Each man harnesses three camels abreast, a female, on which he rides, in the middle, and a male on each side in a leading-rein, and takes care that the female is one who has as recently as possible dropped her young. Their camels are as fast as horses, and much more powerful carriers. There is no need for me to describe the camel, for the Greeks are familiar with what it looks like; one thing, however, I will mention, which will be news to them: the camel in its hind legs has four thighs and four knees, and its genitals point backwards towards its tail. That, then, is how these Indians equip themselves for the expedition, and they plan their time-table so as actually to get their hands on the gold during the hottest part of the day, when the heat will have driven the ants underground. In this part of the world the sun is not, as it is elsewhere, hottest at noon, but in the morning: from dawn, that is, until closing-time in the market. During this part of the day the heat is much fiercer than it is at noon in Greece, and the natives are said to soak themselves in water to make it endurable. At midday the heat diminishes and is much the same here as elsewhere, and, as the afternoon goes on, it becomes about equal to what one finds in other countries in the early morning. Towards evening it grows cooler and cooler, until at sunset it is really cold.

When the Indians reach the place where the gold is, they fill the bags they have brought with them with sand, and start for home again as fast as they can go; for the ants (as is said in the Persians' story) smell them and at once give chase; nothing in the world can touch these ants for speed, so not one of the Indians would get home alive, if they did not make sure of a good start while the ants were mustering their forces. The male camels, who are slower *movers than the females, soon begin to drag and are left behind, one after the other, while the females are kept going hard by the memory of their young, who were left at home.*

According to the Persians, most of the gold is got in the way I have described; they also mine a certain quantity – but not so much – within their own territory.

Herodotus, The Histories, Book 3

Answer

You may be quite amazed.

Discussion

Though it may seem unlikely, this story about the 'ants' seeking gold has latterly been proven to be true. *The Guardian* of 30 November 1996 reported that Michel Peissel, a Frenchman, had spotted marmots burrowing into the sands in the Himalayas; the sands were, in fact, full of gold particles. In making this discovery Peissel said he had done better than both Alexander the Great and Suleiman the Magnificent, who had each been unable to find the gold-seeking ants.

THE ENCIRCLING OCEAN

Greek knowledge of the world was also limited by a rather curious and unproven mythological idea, namely that the earth was surrounded by the stream of Ocean (see Figure 1.6), with its mysterious tides and other non-Mediterranean features; the idea that one might consider crossing this river of Ocean to visit Britain, for instance, was regarded with extreme repugnance, though Pytheas, a sailor from Massilia (Marseilles), does seem to have visited the British Isles c. 300 BCE. On the other hand, people who lived near the surrounding Ocean were thought to be specially favoured by the gods. For example, the Ethiopians (i.e. the present inhabitants of the Sudan) were to be found at the furthest extent of Africa and were dear to the sea-god Poseidon; in northern Europe another semi-legendary people were thought to exist, the Hyperboreans – those who lived beyond the North Wind. In ancient history they seem to have controlled the amber route and were supposed to have regularly sent gifts to Apollo's shrine at Delos.

Of course, this early and rather boxed-in picture of the world was much extended after Alexander's conquests and, during the Roman

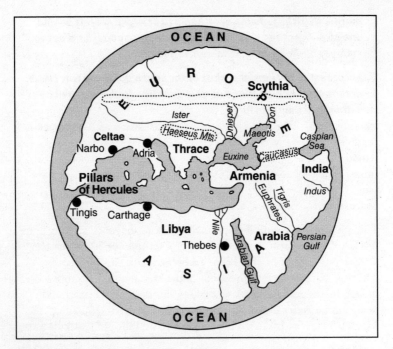

Figure 1.6 The world according to Hecateus c. 500 BCE

period, Greek geographers like Strabo and Ptolemy were able to provide much more in the way of information. One tends to forget that modern map-making skills did not exist and that, even at the end of the Roman period, things had not advanced much further than tables of distances for the practical use of officials and generals.

How do we know about the Greeks?

When Constantinople fell, in 1453 CE, some of the most eminent scholars of Greece emigrated to Venice and the courts of Renaissance Italy, taking their manuscripts of the Greek classics with them and in this way the Greek heritage was transmitted to the West. You must appreciate that little Greek was known in Western Europe before this time. Shortly after this date the copying of the Classical texts in manuscript largely ceased because the invention of printing enabled a wider public access to the Greek authors.

HOW DO WE KNOW THAT WE ARE READING WHAT THE GREEKS ACTUALLY WROTE?

The whole apparatus of Classical scholarship began to take shape during the Renaissance. It was believed that texts which had been transmitted for hundreds of years by the copying of manuscripts were full of mistakes and in some cases hopelessly corrupt. Scholars devoted their lives to solving textual problems, because it was important to establish that one was reading what the author had written. Only then could one move on to dealing with the ideas and implications of the texts. It also became clearer, as knowledge increased, that accidents and also deliberate policies of selection had considerably reduced the stock of literature which had once been available. For example, to look at some famous dramatists, of the estimated 90 plays of Aeschylus only seven have survived, and one of these is now regarded as probably written by his son; similarly, only seven of Sophocles' plays, originally amounting to more than 120 in all, are still in existence.

THE GROWTH OF ARCHAEOLOGY

Many generations had contemplated with wonder and imagination those fragments of Classical civilization that had survived above ground. In certain localities, mainly in Italy, excavation of tombs had contributed to the stock of Greek vases, although in the middle of the eighteenth century these were often regarded not as Greek but as 'Etruscan'.

In the nineteenth century another burst of activity was generated by Heinrich Schliemann, who was the first to excavate at Mycenae and Troy.

Insight

Heinrich Schliemann (1822–90)

Schliemann was a German businessman who made his fortune early and then retired to excavate Homeric sites. He and his assistants worked at Troy from 1870 to 1890, where they found nine cities built one on top of the other. While at Mycenae in 1876 he discovered the shaft graves from a hint in Pausanias' account of the site. He also worked at the citadel of Tiryns in 1884.

Of course, these famous Homeric locations (to be discussed in Chapter 2) were not sites from the Classical period and many scholars were prepared to ridicule Schliemann's efforts at first, thinking that he was naive in assuming that the legendary cities that Homer wrote about had ever really existed. In fact, people are still arguing about the relevance of what Schliemann excavated to Homer's poems; is there any connection? But from this time the new science of archaeology was established and soon moved to replace the haphazard knowledge of the ancient world with a more exact chronological scheme.

This has produced some interesting results in relation to the texts with which we started. At the beginning of the twentieth century it became possible to compare the versions preserved on Egyptian papyri, which had been preserved in the dry climate of the desert since the period when the Greeks and Romans controlled Egypt. We now know that, give or take a few still unsolvable problems, we are reading the same texts as the Ancients. Occasionally new material emerges, for example, private letters and accounts, which gives us new insight into daily life. Only a few new poems, fragments of plays and other literary works have come to light.

10 THINGS TO REMEMBER

1 Greece is more accessible to visitors now than it ever was in the days when most educated people studied Classics.

2 Greece, then and now, needed to trade in order to support its population.

3 The Greeks are best defined as speakers of the Greek language. Speakers of the Greek language have existed from at least 2000 BCE to the present.

4 The Classical period is usually defined as 500–323 BCE. After this the Greeks became part of the Alexandrian, Roman and Byzantine Empires.

5 Greeks lived in city-states.

6 Collectively they called themselves the Hellenes.

7 The Greeks planted daughter-cities, or colonies, round the Mediterranean and Black Sea coasts. They had little knowledge of the interior.

8 Archaeology, which is a comparatively recent science, begins with Heinrich Schliemann.

9 Pottery is the most accurate way of dating Greek sites.

10 Though only the most important manuscripts were preserved and copied, scholars have been able to establish the authenticity of the texts.

Pre-Classical Origins – Mycenae and Pylos

Aim

The aim of this chapter is to demonstrate that the early phases of Greek society are important because they underlie the culture of later times. The epic poems that seem to refer back to this prehistoric age were a constant point of reference in the thinking process of many people during the later periods. After reading this chapter you should be able to answer some of the following questions.

▶ Why was the past perceived in terms of myth and legend?
▶ How did this view express itself in literature?
▶ What was the appearance of Nestor's palace?
▶ What is its possible relation to Homer's *Odyssey*?
▶ How much does Hesiod know about the past and how does he express his knowledge?

A guide to the pronunciation of important names in this chapter.

HOMER (*home-err* with stress on the first syllable). Epic poet whose work became revered as a guide to conduct. The principal texts attributed to Homer are *The Iliad* and *The Odyssey*. The world they deal with is that of the Trojan War, which the Greeks thought had taken place about 1250 BCE. We now think the poems were written down c. 725 BCE.

HESIOD (*hee-see-odd* with the stress on '*hee*'). One of the earliest poets c. 700 BCE. Author of *Works and Days*.

MYCENAE (*my-seen-ee* with the stress on the second syllable). City near Argos with extensive Bronze Age remains. Note that the word 'Mycenaean' refers to the civilization at the end of this period, not just to the city.

TIRYNS (*ti* [short i] -*rins* with the stress on the first syllable). Neighbouring fortified citadel.

PYLOS (*pie-loss* with the stress on the first syllable). Name of a town in southern Peloponnese, and formerly of a district associated with Nestor.

TELEMACHUS (*tell-em-ack-us* with stress on the second syllable). Son of Odysseus. At the beginning of the *The Odyssey* he goes to look for his father and arrives at a place called 'sandy Pylos'.

The lost world of the Mycenaeans

Let us begin at the emergence of Greece from the Dark Ages in approximately 800 BCE. At the end of Chapter 1 I described the ways in which knowledge of the Greeks has come down to us. These were, briefly, the study of texts and the science of archaeology.

Which of these methods would the Greeks of 800–700 BCE have been able to use to explore their own past?

Answer

Neither.

Discussion

There were no texts; the art of writing was in the process of being invented. The science of archaeology dates from the nineteenth century CE. Of course, nothing can be as simple as that.

Insight

In the timeline on the walls of the passageway connecting the terminals at Heathrow Airport, London, the Greeks begin at 800 BCE. Do you think this can be true?

MEMORIES OF THE HEROIC AGE

There were plenty of stories and oral traditions about the past in circulation: the first literature – the poetry of Homer and Hesiod – was an attempt to organize these myths and legends and to write them down. Similarly, we assume, the Greeks tried to come to terms with the remains of the past that are visible as objects and historic sites. We don't know what had survived from earlier periods in terms of material culture. Certainly the Greeks don't seem to have deliberately dug in the ground to find evidence of the past, but some sites were clearly visible above ground, such as Mycenae and Tiryns, and there were large tombs inviting exploration or robbery. Because of the large stones used in their construction they were thought to be the work of Cyclopean.

Homer

Homer's epic poems, *The Iliad* and *The Odyssey*, are so full of good stories and poetic inventiveness that some people feel that they have never really been surpassed. Their origins are one of the great discussion points of Classical studies. They are written in an early form of the Greek language, but because of the mixture of dialects we cannot say with confidence that it was a real language that anybody actually spoke. In fact, rather the reverse is probably the case; it seems to have been a special language that was used only in these poems. If, as is now thought, Homer's poems reached their present form in the eighth century BCE, then there seems to be no way, in the absence of writing and other methods of recording events, in which he could have had any substantial knowledge of the past and, in particular, of the Mycenaean period, which was at its height so many years before. (See the time chart in Chapter 1 to refresh your memory.) But there are some mysterious coincidences that are difficult to account for.

One or two objects from the past are described in Homer's poems as if they were great treasures. These valuable items may have been handed down to his generation as heirlooms, or the Greeks may have opened tombs to give honours to the heroes they thought were buried there and so discovered them; it is also known that, later, a certain amount of military equipment was hung up in temples. Such objects were often associated with heroic or legendary persons. It is from Homer's poetry that we know so much about who some of these heroic individuals were and what they did.

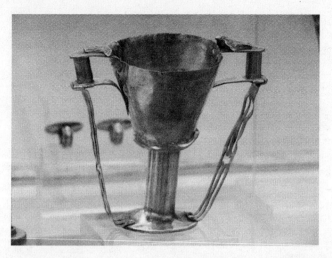

Figure 2.1 Nestor's cup. Gold. Approximately 15 cm (6 inches) high. Found by Schliemann in the fourth shaft grave at Mycenae. It was given its name because of its supposed resemblance to the object described in the Iliad text

NESTOR'S CUP

Let us try to put the points in the above discussion in order and follow them through. Here is an example, taken from *The Iliad*, which is set at the time of the legendary Trojan War, traditionally dated by the Greeks to between 1250 and 1000 BCE. It describes a cup belonging to a hero called Nestor.

> *She began by moving up to them a handsome polished table with enamelled legs. On this she put a bronze dish with an onion to flavour the drink, some yellow honey, and sacred barley-meal; and beside these a magnificent beaker adorned with golden studs, which the old man had brought from home. It had four handles. Each was supported by two legs; and on top of each, facing one another, a pair of golden doves were feeding. Anyone else would have found it difficult to shift the beaker from the table when it was full, but Nestor, old as he was, could lift it without trouble. In this cup, their comely attendant mixed them the pottage with Pramnian wine, and after making it ready by grating into it some goat's milk cheese with a bronze grater and sprinkling white barley on top, she invited them to drink, which they did.*
>
> *Iliad*, Book 11, 627–37

What would you need to do to convince yourself that Schliemann was making a correct identification? What are the resemblances? What are the differences?

Discussion

You would need to check on the dates and provenance of the object; dating first. The contents of the grave at Mycenae were deposited in the sixteenth century BCE; the deposit was then sealed until it was discovered by Schliemann in the nineteenth century CE. So the object is about 300 years older than the supposed date of Nestor, assuming that he was a real person and lived at the alleged time of the Trojan War. Nor could it have been seen by Homer or any of the Greeks.

Chronological table of the above discussion; of course, all dates are approximate.

1600–1500 BCE	The cup was made.
1500 BCE	It was deposited in a grave and sealed before this date.
1300 BCE	Birth of Nestor (earliest possible date).
1250 BCE	Trojan War, where Nestor drinks from his cup.
c. 725 BCE	Homer's poems are written down.

The resemblances between text and object are quite striking at first, especially because it has golden nails at the foot and there are two doves (though not four as in the poem); it is not quite clear what is meant by 'the two legs', but the metalwork is unusual. But the poem also seems to make a great point about the weight of Nestor's cup, *so that it must have been considerably larger in size and cannot be the object in the museum.*

So much, you might say, for Schliemann; but I think that scholars who jeer at Schliemann are being unfair. Of course, he appeared to be over-enthusiastic about this and similar discoveries, but it is remarkable that any details of the object are in the poem at all. One explanation, which would involve us in a long detour, is that Homer's poems are the end product of a long oral tradition; this might mean that the early versions of the poem were by people who had seen such a cup in the sixteenth century BCE. Over the years the poets exaggerated the size of the treasure.

Another explanation is that such objects continued to be made – in the craft tradition – and that even in Homer's day something similar could still be seen which he was able to describe.

The site of Mycenae

Let us now move to consider the site where the cup was found. Today everybody knows something about the world of the people whom we call the Mycenaeans. Every primary school child knows more than Homer and his audience, and more than any of the later Greeks. The gold masks which covered the faces of their dead kings and the enormous structures that still stand above ground level in various parts of Greece fascinate us as much as the similar golden tomb-furnishings of Tutankhamun and the pyramids and temples of ancient Egypt. All we can say is that the Greeks of the eighth century BCE had some inkling of the glories of this past epoch, even though it had existed centuries before, and there had been an intervening Dark Age when much destruction by war and earthquake, together with confusing movements of population, had taken place. Some sites were impossible to ignore because they were identified in legends and in the epic poems of Homer. Agamemnon, the leader of the Greek forces at Troy, was King of 'Mycenae, rich in gold'. More importantly, Mycenae, although it later became impoverished, continued to be inhabited. It was never completely buried or lost to human knowledge. Figure 2.2 is a plan of the site; this may well figure in a tour of the Peloponnese on your Greek holiday.

What are we looking at here? You should forget Homer and Agamemnon for a minute; what could modern archaeology say about this site?

Answer

This is a Bronze Age site and it was inhabited through most of the second millennium BCE.

Discussion

What we are looking at is the citadel, which you can think of as a fortified town. In this it resembles many other Bronze Age sites, such as Troy; or you could compare with a castle surviving from

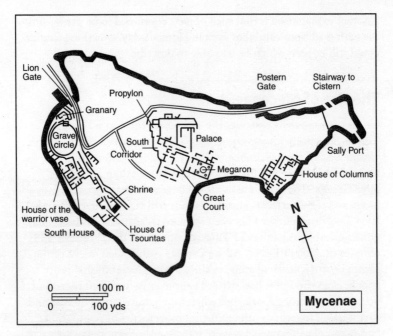

Figure 2.2 Site plan of Mycenae. Notice the sally port on the far side from the main gate and the entrance to the underground water supply

the Middle Ages. It is surrounded by a defensive wall, which in some places takes considerable advantage from the lie of the land as it skirts the appropriately named Chaos gorge. In other places it approaches flat land and one must assume outworks and additional defences would be needed. The whole of the Argive Plain is scattered with other Mycenaean structures, which may have been outworks in a defensive system. The central section at the top of the 'castle' of Mycenae would have been the royal palace. A number of houses are included in the walled area together with the Grave Circle near the gate. This is where the shaft graves were found. If we study the chronological development of the site it is clear that the walls were extended and that these comparatively early graves were deliberately enclosed within the perimeter, perhaps because their relation to the living involved status.

Outside the walls are the various structures known to the Greeks as the 'treasuries' of Atreus and others, which we now know to be colossal beehive tombs and which were erected at a later period than the shaft graves. We have no idea who was buried in them.

Judging by the surviving evidence the richest period in the history of the site would seem to have been about 1600 BCE when the people who were buried in the shaft graves were loaded with treasures.

Homer and his picture of early society

What would life have been like at a Mycenaean palace, according to heroic legend? Here is an extract from Homer's other poem, *The Odyssey*, describing the arrival of Telemachus, the son of Odysseus, at Nestor's palace. It is said to be situated at Pylos, in the Southern Peloponnese, but Homer's poems give no clear indication of where Pylos was. The modern holiday town is in a quite different situation; it was formerly called Navarino and the enclosed bay in front of it was the site of a famous battle in 1827 CE.

His prayer reached the ears of Pallas Athene; and now the Gerenian charioteer Nestor led the way towards his stately home, followed by his sons and his daughters' husbands. When they came to the royal palace, they took their places on the settles and chairs, and the old man prepared a bowl of mellow wine for his guests, from a jar that had stood for ten years before the maid undid the cap and broached it. When the old king had mixed a bowl of this vintage, he poured a little out, with earnest prayers to Athene, Daughter of Zeus who wears the aegis.

They made their libations and quenched their thirst, after which the rest went off to their several quarters for the night. But the Gerenian horseman Nestor arranged for King Odysseus' son Telemachus to sleep at the palace itself, on a wooden bedstead in the echoing portico, with Peisistratus beside him; for that young spearman and captain was the only unmarried son left to him in the home. The king himself retired to rest in his room at the back of the high building, where the queen his wife made bed and bedding ready for him.

When tender Dawn had brushed the sky with her rose-tinted hands, Gerenian Nestor got up from his bed, went out and seated himself on a smooth bench of white marble, which stood, gleaming with polish, in front of his lofty doors. Here Neleus once

*had sat and proved himself a rival of the gods in wisdom; but he
had long since met his doom and gone to Hades' Halls. So now
Gerenian Nestor sat there in his turn, sceptre in hand, a Warden
of the Achaean race. His sons all came from their rooms and
gathered round him, Echephron and Stratius, Perseus and Aretus,
and the noble Thrasymedes. The young lord Peisistratus came last
and made the sixth. Prince Telemachus was ushered to a seat at
their side ...*

*In the meantime, the beautiful Polycaste, King Nestor's youngest
daughter, had given Telemachus his bath. When she had bathed
him and rubbed him with olive oil, she gave him a tunic and
arranged a fine cloak round his shoulders, so that he stepped out
of the bath looking like an immortal god. He then went and sat
down by Nestor, the shepherd of the people.*

Odyssey, Book 3, 385–99 and 464–9

*Even from these short extracts you can see the luxury of life in the
Heroic Age. (In Homer's time the evidence is that such luxury was
not readily available.) How do you account for these descriptions?*

Answer

You could simply say that they are poetic and imaginative fancies
about life in the past, so much better than in the present. It is just like
a fairy story.

The site of Nestor's palace

The above answer would have been perfectly fair until 1939 when the
American archaeologist Carl Blegen began to excavate the recently
discovered site of 'Nestor's palace' at a position approximately 13 km
(8 miles) north of Pylos.

ITS DESTRUCTION

The palace had been destroyed about 1200 BCE. It was burnt down
and completely buried and was, therefore, unknown to Homer and
the later Greeks. Figure 2.3 is a reconstruction of the richly decorated
interior, and Figure 2.4 is the bathtub.

The whole impact of the site is quite overwhelming. Homer was not
exaggerating in his descriptions of Mycenaean society. In some sense
the legends seem to incorporate details of a real past.

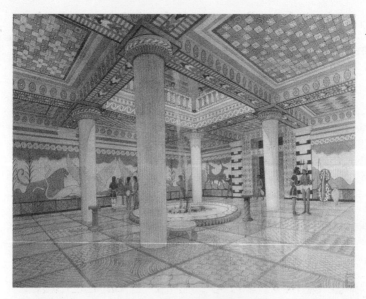

Figure 2.3 Interior of palace at Pylos. Sketch based on archaeological evidence by Piet De Jong

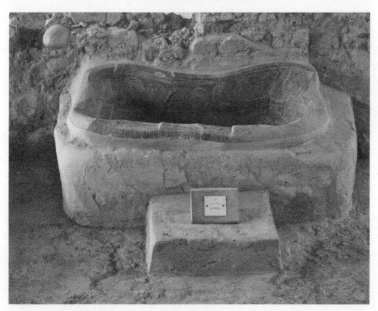

Figure 2.4 The bath at Pylos

> **Insight**
>
> Linear B is the name of a script used at this time; it was inscribed on clay tablets and combined pictograms and syllabic forms. The language of the tablets was deciphered by Michael Ventris in the early 1950s and was found to be an early form of Greek.

We know little about the inhabitants of these palaces but we know they did speak Greek because of the evidence of Linear B tablets. The fire that destroyed Pylos served to bake the clay tablets, which were used by the 'accountants' in their room at the front of the palace; the tablets contained lists of stores and equipment, the amount of wheat that could be obtained from each estate and lists of people who were presumably slaves. We are given a picture of a centralized bureaucratic society, which is quite different from that of later Greece or that portrayed in Homer's poems. Similar tablets have since been found at other Mycenaean sites.

THE DARK AGES

After the destruction of Pylos and most of the other Mycenaean sites there is a period of approximately 200 years about which little is known. When settlements are again established the quality of life shown in the evidence is poor indeed. In particular, the art of writing disappeared completely. When it was reintroduced from Phoenicia in the eighth century BCE the Greeks adopted an alphabet and began to use letters as we do, rather than syllabic forms.

Hesiod and the world of the eighth century BCE

We next move on to Hesiod, a poet who may have been contemporary with Homer, writing about 700 BCE. In his most famous poem, *Works and Days*, his subject is life in the present. Occasionally, he too looks backwards and tries to explain how the world has arrived in its present state.

Read and think about the meaning of the following extract from Hesiod. He has been describing the course of human history, presumably as it has been handed down to him. Hesiod uses the vocabulary and approach of mythology. There have been five Ages. First he describes the Golden Age – a time of abundance – and a Silver Age, when the human race was childish. Then came the Age of Bronze:

And Zeus the father made a race of bronze,   *143*
Sprung from the ash tree, worse than the silver race,
But strange and full of power. And they loved
The groans and violence of war; they ate
No bread; their hearts were flinty-hard; they were
Terrible men; their strength was great, their arms
And shoulders and their limbs invincible.

Their weapons were of bronze, their houses bronze;   *150*
Their tools were bronze: black iron was not known.

They died by their own hands, and nameless, went
To Hades' chilly house. Although they were
Great soldiers, they were captured by black Death,
And left the shining brightness of the sun.

But when this race was covered by the earth,
The son of Kronos made another, fourth
Upon the fruitful land, more just and good,
A godlike race of heroes, who are called
The demi-gods – the race before our own.   *160*

Foul wars and dreadful battles ruined some;
Some sought the flocks of Oedipus, and died
In Cadmus' land, at seven-gated Thebes;
And some, who crossed the open sea in ships,
For fair-haired Helen's sake, were killed at Troy.

These men were covered up in death, but Zeus
The son of Kronos gave the others life
And homes apart from mortals, at Earth's edge.

And there they live a carefree life, beside
The whirling Ocean, on the Blessed Isles.   *170*

Three times a year the blooming, fertile earth
Bears honeyed fruits for them, the happy ones.

And Kronos is their king, far from the gods,
For Zeus released him from his bonds, and these,
The race of heroes, well deserve their fame.

Far-seeing Zeus then made another race,
The fifth, who live now on the fertile earth.

> *I wish I were not of this race, that I*
> *Had died before, or had not yet been born.*

> *This is the race of iron.* 180

Make notes on the three stages in the extract. Considering that we have assumed that the early Greeks knew little of their past, it is remarkable what Hesiod has received from myth.

Can you match these phases with the archaeological periods of Greek culture listed in the chronological table on in Chapter 1?

Caution

It is tempting to rush in and equate Hesiod's 'race of bronze' with the Greek Bronze Age of modern archaeology; likewise 'race of iron' with the Iron Age. In fact, these terms were not used in the archaeological sense until the nineteenth century CE. I concede that you could point to lines 150–1 to show that Hesiod is referring to the use of metals.

But is this what the whole sequence is about?

Discussion

Hesiod's main purpose is to inform us that in the course of time things have steadily deteriorated (there is something rather ironical about this as we know that Hesiod is at the beginning of the period of progress in knowledge and the arts which we identify as the height of the Greek achievement). The Golden Age obviously doesn't mean that everyday objects were made of gold, nor does the Silver Age refer to the use of that metal. They are metaphorical terms and, I suspect, go back further than Hesiod, because he is a traditional poet like most poets in early societies.

There was no desire for originality in our sense and, as we have seen with Homer, poetry reproduced forms and ideas from the past; however, earlier writing on the subject is not available to us and so we owe it to Hesiod when we use these terms about periods in history. Therefore, to Hesiod the Bronze Age is worse because it is more violent than the Silver Age and is, therefore, to be associated with a cheaper metal; did you notice, however, that, although he lives in the Age of Iron, he knows that bronze was used for armour and weapons? You might want to think about how he knows this; I will keep a possible answer back for the moment. The Iron

Age – Hesiod's present – is pretty appalling, one gathers, and is going to get worse. Obviously Hesiod is a pessimist.

What has been left out in this discussion of the extract?

Answer and discussion

Quite a lot; it is amazing how much is packed into these lines. Between the Bronze and Iron Ages comes the unexpected – the phase of the heroes or demi-gods. I say 'unexpected' because we have not been led to expect anything like this from the general downward drift of Hesiod's gloomy narrative. Obviously he couldn't leave this out to fit his thesis because it was so well known; as opposed to the other ages, individuals are named. He presumably knew about some of these from Homer, who would also have informed him that the early soldiers fought with 'the pitiless bronze'. So this is once again a reference to the Heroic Age of Greek legend; he may well have had other oral sources, lost to us, as the stories were widespread in the culture of the time. Later on you will notice that many Greek plays refer to these well-known individuals, for example, Agamemnon, and the stories were used again and again on vases and as the subject for sculpture.

Further study of Hesiod is useful, because he gives us a realistic picture of early Greece. In spite of his rather dour vision of the world, Hesiod is worth following up because his *Works and Days*, from which the extract was taken, provides a kind of farmer's calendar and helps one to visualize the simplicity of agricultural life. The *Theogony*, his other surviving poem, deals with the successive generations of the gods. This brings us to Chapter 3 and our next subject.

10 THINGS TO REMEMBER

1 There is an early phase of Greek civilization, usually called the Mycenaean period.

2 Because we can use archaeological methods of research we know more about Bronze Age society than the Greeks of the Classical period did.

3 Homer is not a reliable source for this period as he relied on heroic legends.

4 In so far as the Homeric poems are the product of a long oral tradition, handed down by 'singers', some elements of history are preserved.

5 An example is the description of Nestor's palace in the *Odyssey,* which seems to match a site excavated near Pylos in 1939.

6 Clay tablets were found with writing in Linear B script. They contained the records of a bureaucracy.

7 This society was destroyed about 1200 BCE. A period called the Dark Ages followed.

8 In about 700 BCE the poet Hesiod gives us a picture of a much grimmer society.

9 In *Works and Days* he offers an account of earlier history, and tells us that he lives in the Age of Iron.

10 His approach to history is mythological.

3

Cult and Religion – Olympia and Delphi

Aim

At the end of this chapter you should be able to discuss some of the questions below, although it must be made clear at the outset that the evidence for the more secret aspects of Greek religious beliefs has never been available and can only be inferred.

▶ As opposed to the official religion, how can we find out about practices of the peasants and ordinary people's beliefs?
▶ Can you distinguish between the private and public aspects of Greek religion?
▶ Why did the Greeks meet at Olympia?
▶ What happened at Delphi?

A guide to the pronunciation of important names in this chapter.

OLYMPIA (*o-lim-pi-a* with the stress on the second syllable). Presumably because of the cult of Zeus who was known as 'Olympian Zeus' from his home on Mount Olympus. This is in a different part of Greece.

DELPHI (*del-fee* with stress on the first syllable). Sacred site in central Greece.

CROESUS (*kree-sus* with stress on the first syllable). King of Lydia in the sixth century BCE.

OMPHALOS (stress on the first syllable). The Greek word for 'navel', a round stone at Delphi that was regarded as the centre of the earth.

Cult and religion

Did you notice a rosary and various religious pictures in the cab of your Greek bus-driver? Did he mutter to himself as you went through an earthquake zone? Did you notice wayside shrines devoted to the victims of road accidents? Some aspects of Greek religion seem so ancient that they may be regarded as the primitive superstitions of the Mediterranean area, and may have antedated the arrival of the Greeks. Certain practices among the peasantry relating to the evil eye, for example, or the wearing of amulets, still continue to this day despite the apparent victory of the Orthodox Church in Greece and of Catholicism and Islam in the rest of the region. They must always have existed, although they have largely gone unnoticed in Classical Greek literature.

In the Bronze Age gallery of the British Museum you can see tiny ceramic models of human arms, legs and joints found in a Mycenaean shrine. These are offerings to acknowledge help received in the cure of some physical affliction; a model of the part of the body affected, for example, ear, eyes or limbs, is dedicated to the god. Even today you can still see pictures like these hanging up at places where there is believed to be healing or cure for disease.

EARLY STAGES OF RELIGION

This primitive stage of religion may have been restricted to small areas and specific localities, and the devotions seem to be purely personal. There does not seem to have been a priesthood as such in early Greek religion, but members of families engaged in other occupations looked after local shrines and cult objects. An individual prayed for help and made an appropriate sacrifice, usually of an animal or bird, according to his or her means. Our earliest evidence of Greek religion in literature (Homer) indicates clearly the necessity of frequent sacrifice to keep on the right side of the gods. A bargain was struck and supposed to be kept – those who honoured the gods were rewarded.

TEMPLE AND CULT

The next stage – of organized religion – is probably to be dated from the appearance of the *temenos*, or sacred plot of land, which contained an altar.

From the seventh century BCE there is the first evidence of temples and sacrifices outside them. This, in turn, would generate a class of priests and priestesses together with temple officials. The Greeks thought that such practices had come from the Near East, but note that the temple officials were not to be compared with the powerful priests of ancient Egypt.

These temples were quite simple in their layout. The interior contained the treasury where the property belonging to the god was stored and the *cella* (enclosed room) where the image of the god was kept out of public view. Access to this sanctuary would have been strictly controlled and the door from it to the outside world was normally opened only on special feast days, so that the image could 'see' the sacrifice performed outside. Cult practices are difficult to establish, but in many centres an annual procession took place; the image might then be appropriately dressed and taken on a tour of the locality, perhaps to establish boundaries, or festivals and games might be held in honour of the god, serving to proclaim a sense of social identity. The Olympic Games performed the latter function and showed honour to Zeus.

The site of Olympia

Any archaeological tour of the Peloponnese will take you to Olympia. This is a large site and most of it can be reconstructed (see Figure 3.1). Most everybody has heard of Olympia because of the Olympic Games. The picture shows how, over a period of time, the area was laid out with temples, assembly halls and semireligious buildings, together with altars and statues associated with the victors.

How does Olympia differ from the stadium or leisure centre that you know best?

Answer

The stress does not seem to be on the sporting facilities.

Discussion

The temples and religious buildings would have dominated early Olympia: a lot of the features shown here are as late as Roman times.

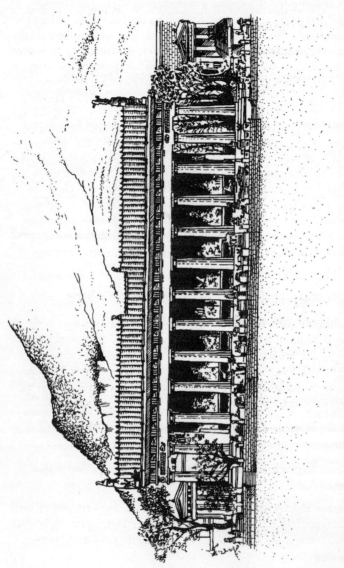

Figure 3.1 A reconstruction of the sanctuary at Olympia, thronged with statues dedicated by victorious athletes. (A photograph showing part of Olympia today appears in Chapter 10)

The reason the Greeks assembled here every four years was to honour Zeus. These games began in 776 BCE and Greek dates were registered from this date time; for example, something was said to have happened 'in the sixteenth Olympiad'.

If you were successful in a race or other sport you might be honoured with a statue, or some other commemoration in stone; or your praises would be sung by a chorus, which would have been trained by a composer who had also written the verses (see *The Praise Singer* by Mary Renault in the booklist at the end of the book for an imaginative account of the career of Simonides). Many of the early Greek lyric poets earned a living in this way; later, a famous writer of choral odes called Pindar (c. 522 BCE–c. 440 BCE) became a kind of poet-in-residence at these and other games and sang of the victor's city, often in myths honouring the gods who had given the athlete his physical strength.

It is time that we considered the use of myth and the place of the gods in Greek religion.

Mythology and mythological explanations

Myth has been referred to several times as a characteristic of early Greek ideas about the world, and I have suggested that in many ways this was an approach inherited from the Egyptians and the peoples of the Middle East. Some aspects of Hesiod's tales are paralleled in Babylonian and other Mesopotamian myths. I have to assume some general knowledge of Greek and other mythical stories here.

What do we mean by the word 'myth'? What are the main characteristics of mythical stories which distinguish them from other narratives?

Answer

This is not an easy question. The word 'myth' is most frequently used in colloquial English to mean an untrue story. Though this isn't what we mean here, it is a useful start because it helps us to understand that a myth-story

▶ is usually odd and unexpected
▶ involves the supernatural, i.e. the relations of gods with the world of men and women

▶ explains at a simple level why the world is as it is, or how it works, and the explanations are, generally speaking, 'religious' as opposed to 'scientific'.

An example

During a walk in the country, thunder and lightning may cause panic. The myth tells you that Zeus is angry. Thunder and lightning are the aural and visual aspects of the sky-god throwing his thunderbolts. You may still be frightened, but at least you feel secure because you know what is happening. (Perhaps the scientific explanation of these atmospheric phenomena has the same effect!)

Therefore, in the early stages of Greek society, religion does not seem to have been a unitary system of belief but a collection of myths; some of these myths may contradict others, because they have originated at different times or in different places; what we call Greek religion is really an amalgam of local cults. Homer and Hesiod seem to have been responsible for the first attempts to systematize the principal myths and to present the Greek world with a kind of theology.

THE GODS

There are twelve principal gods, most of whom live on Mount Olympus, ruled by father Zeus. Mount Olympus is in northern Greece.

The twelve Olympian gods, as shown on the Parthenon frieze, which is a fair indication of their comparative status in Classical times.

Zeus – ruler of the gods, father of gods and men
Poseidon – his brother, god of the sea and of earthquakes
Hermes – messenger of the gods
Hera – Zeus's consort, very powerful
Aphrodite – goddess of love
Athena – goddess of the intellectual arts, patroness of Athens
Apollo – god of the sun, light and healing
Artemis – his sister, goddess of hunting, and protector of wild animals
Demeter – goddess of corn and fertility
Hephaestus – god of metalworking and associated crafts

Ares – god of war
Dionysus – god of wine, and drama.

Other important gods were:

Eos – goddess of the dawn
Gaia or **Ge** (pronounced *Gee* with a hard *g*) – ancient primeval goddess of the earth
Hades – god of the dead and the underworld
Hestia – goddess of the hearth, originally one of the twelve, until she was replaced by Dionysos. She was rather unexciting mythologically as she was confined to the house.

Hesiod's *Theogony* attempted to explain the generations of the gods and their inter-relationships. Later authors largely agreed with him but sometimes contributed different links. This network of divine unions and their offspring is best conveyed by a diagram – see Figure 3.2.

The primeval void was called Chaos – hence 'the reign of Chaos and old Night' in Milton. When things sorted themselves out the two principal entities were Ouranos (the Sky) and Gaia (the Earth). These produced many groups of gods and monsters, of whom the Titans were the most important. The youngest Titan – Cronos – eventually rebelled against his father and supplanted him. During his rule humankind enjoyed a Golden Age.

It had been prophesied that Cronos would be overthrown by one of his children, so he swallowed them as soon as they were born. His wife Rhea hid herself in a cave in Crete where she gave birth to Zeus. When Zeus reached maturity he was able to free his brothers and sisters from inside their father, and a new war began between Cronos and the Titans on the one hand and Zeus and the Olympians on the other. Zeus and the new generation of gods were successful, but the story hints that even Zeus may be overthrown in some distant future (see Aeschylus' *Prometheus Bound*).

Insight

Some of the more lugubrious detail of this account sounds more Middle Eastern than Greek, and it is not entirely clear how much of this rather grotesque 'theology' was of great importance. We find it strange that the behaviour of the gods towards each other – and towards humans – was unpredictable; the main difference between the gods and humans would seem to be that the gods are immortal.

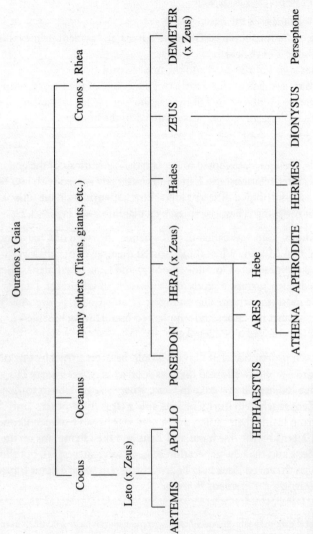

Figure 3.2 The generations of the gods

Belief in the gods must be taken as universal, but they were not above criticism. As time went on attempts were made to order the behaviour of the gods so that it was more seemly, and in the fifth century philosophers were concerned to point out that the poets such as Homer were misleading people. Socrates felt that the gods could never cause misery and harm to each other or to humans.

Insight

A word of caution is necessary here. The fact that a few individuals seem to challenge accepted beliefs has obviously been singled out for praise by Christian commentators at a much later stage, in the same way that the Pharaoh Akhenaton has been promoted for his monotheistic heresies (which were obliterated from Egyptian temples).

It is necessary to make an effort to appreciate what life under polytheism must have been like. Gods could be played off one against the other; people must have been influenced in their choice of which god to solicit by the situation they were attempting to live through. Therefore there was a special goddess, Eileithyia, who gave help during childbirth, for example; she does not seem to have been part of the Olympian set-up and is now thought to go back to the Minoan period.

Insight

Minoan refers to the civilization of the early Bronze Age period, based upon Crete. It preceded the Mycenaeans, who seem to have inherited a great deal of Minoan culture.

Furthermore, individuals may well have felt that they were under the protection of a particular god. This is well illustrated in the *Odyssey* where Odysseus is specially favoured by Athena.

MINOR DEITIES

Lower down the scale, every wood and valley had its nymphs or other rural deities – with limited powers usually connected with the fertility of the area.

Then came demi-gods, members of the human race with a divine parent, and heroes, those who had earned immortality by some supreme achievement. Sometimes the achievement is also the record of a disaster as in the myth of Orion.

Orion was a giant huntsman of divine descent; he was either the son or the grandson of the sea-god Poseidon, who gave him a special gift: he could walk on the sea. Orion was such a good hunter that he threatened to kill all the animals upon the earth; therefore the goddess of the earth, Gaia, sent out a huge scorpion which stung him to death. So Zeus put him among the stars as a reward for his prowess, together with the scorpion.

Unfortunately, this isn't the only version. We are told about his relations with women. The story goes on to say that his wife, Side (two syllables), was so beautiful that she rivalled Hera, the most important of the goddesses. For this Side was punished by being thrown down into Tartarus, a deep prison in the underworld. Later Orion was loved by Eos, the goddess of the dawn, who took him to Delos. Finally, Orion attempted to rape the goddess Artemis, or caused her some annoyance; Homer tells us that Artemis acted on behalf of all the gods who resented the liaison with Eos. Therefore, Artemis made a scorpion attack Orion so that he died from its bite. As a result the Scorpion was turned into a constellation and can be seen in the sky; next to it is the giant figure of Orion, who is running for his life.

What do you make of this myth?

Discussion

The first paragraph does make some sense, but it is a very honed-down version of the myth. A number of other things seem to be going on in the second paragraph, and I have put them together into a kind of life story.

(Some selection and editing of these early narratives is unavoidable.) Orion and the Scorpion are still known to us as the constellations with the same names and it is not difficult to imagine people telling stories about the figures they could see in the night sky. This explains the Scorpion's role, so that we have a linking of two constellations.

The rest is more difficult and depends upon how much you already know. Orion and Side are both giants, though they don't feature in the principal legend about the giants as a group, which is that the giants collectively challenged the Olympian gods to battle and were defeated. This looks like some kind of sideshow. Both of these giants are separately destroyed by Olympian gods, Hera and Artemis, for their presumption.

Looking back over all the material, there is some kind of morality here, and it doesn't just apply to giants. You must not go beyond what is reasonable; hunt if you wish, but don't try to kill everything. Don't challenge the gods in a beauty contest, and don't declare war on heaven or make violent attacks upon the Olympian gods.

A MORE COMPLEX MYTH

Orion is not, in fact, an important figure in Greek mythology, but I had to begin by choosing a figure with a comparatively limited range of references. The trouble is that as soon as you say this you have an awful feeling that Orion, so dominant in the heavens, must have had enormous significance at some earlier time but was supplanted in a new phase of religious belief.

Now let us turn to a more famous story which has deeper meanings.

The story of Pandora

Hesiod tells this story twice over: this is the first version in the *Works and Days*.

In the early days of the world Zeus was angry with the demi-gods, Prometheus and his brother Epimetheus, because Prometheus had stolen fire from heaven and given it to men. Zeus therefore instructed Hephaestus to make a woman out of earth and water; the different gods each gave the woman a gift. Athene, patroness of weaving, clothed her; the Graces gave her jewellery and the Hours gave her all the flowers of the spring. Hermes gave her the power of speech but he also put into her a deceitful mind. As every god had given her gifts they called the woman Pandora, because she had everything; but some of the gifts were not what they seemed.

Up to this time men had lived without disease and sickness. But the woman removed the lid of a jar releasing diseases, plagues and evils upon the world of men. Only Hope remained in the jar.

(This is Hesiod's story in the *Works and Days*: other versions say that Pandora brought the jar or box. It contained the gifts of the gods which were all lost except Hope.)

Hesiod's second version (in the *Theogony*) is more elaborate in its descriptions but omits the jar altogether. The evil thing is Pandora herself, and from her are descended the race of women. The moral is that Zeus made woman to be an evil to man.

COMMENT

While misogyny is always with us, Hesiod obviously likes the details of the story as much as the moral he draws from it. You should have noted that Zeus, unlike the principal gods of some religious systems, is quite capable of acting in a nasty and underhand way. Therefore – and most early Greek stories bear this out – you must keep on the right side of Zeus and the other gods by performing due sacrifices and not offending them; if you cheat the gods or draw attention to yourself you will be punished.

The other problem with the story is that it is not clear in the original version where the jar has come from; it is rather like jars in the Arabian Nights stories which happen to contain genii. Therefore, later versions have attempted to tidy this up by having Pandora bring the box or jar with her; but this, like all alterations to these archetypal stories, doesn't necessarily make things easier, because then Zeus is made primarily responsible for the introduction of disease and suffering. Hesiod carefully avoids saying this, and in his second version makes it clear that the origin of evil is woman herself.

Omens and oracles

OMENS

We have already noted the duty of sacrifice. Attached to this was the practice of examining the entrails of the slaughtered animals; in Xenophon's *The Persian Expedition* 2:1 the Greek soldiers are in extreme difficulties; they are cut off in the middle of the Persian

Empire and the problem is partly resolved by consulting the entrails of sacrificed animals. In the next chapter Clearchos says:

> **My friends, when I was sacrificing with a view to marching against the King, the signs were not propitious. This was natural enough; for, as I now understand, between us and the King there is a navigable river, the Tigris. We could not cross this river without boats, and we have no boats. We certainly cannot stay here, because there is no possibility of obtaining supplies. However, when it was a question of making our way to Cyrus's friends, the signs from the sacrifices were extraordinarily favourable.**

I think the remarkable thing is that this is accepted without question as the best way to proceed. A message from the gods has been given.

ORACLES

Similar advice was to be obtained from oracles, which existed at certain well-known sites in Greece; many of these dealt with individual medical queries, and we shall pursue aspects of this at Epidaurus. At Dodona in northern Greece was the oracle of Zeus; here the rustling of the leaves of the sacred oak, or sometimes doves who were sitting in the tree, provided answers to the questions of the inquirers.

Delphi

Delphi was one of the most important oracles and seems to have specialized in political inquiries. The site was sacred to Apollo, who had killed a large snake – the Python – at this place; this symbolized the triumph of reason over the 'dark forces' of the world. Barbarians who tried to loot the sanctuary were allegedly frightened off by divine apparitions. In its remote and shut-in valley, Delphi was supposed to be the *omphalos* or navel of the earth, the true centre of the world. A round stone marked the spot.

Like Olympia it was in a sense neutral territory, and the various city-states put up buildings here to indicate their debt to Apollo and to show off their power and prestige. If you visit Delphi you will find that one or two of these buildings, called treasuries, have been partly restored.

The oracle could be consulted by private persons as well as the representatives of cities. After undergoing the rites of purification

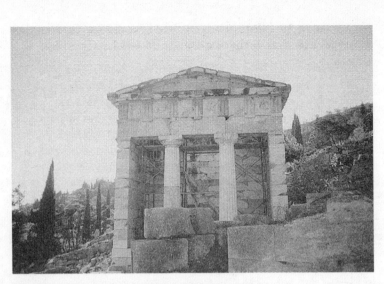

Figure 3.3 Delphi – view from within the Sacred Precinct

in the Castalian Spring the inquirer would put a question to the priests. This was then conveyed to the inner sanctum where the priestess was reputed to intoxicate herself with laurel leaves which she chewed or burnt, or by sitting on a tripod which was perched over a cleft in the rocks; from here a poisonous vapour issued which also may have had a disorientating effect. In her trance the priestess gibbered and muttered a fragmentary reply which was set in order by the priests and delivered in writing, often apparently in witty and memorable verse.

Like Olympia, the oracle seems to have come into being in the eighth century BCE, although it is supposed to have been consulted in earlier periods, according to the stories and dramas about early Greek heroes such as Oedipus; its height of political power was from the sixth to the third century. At this time all major decisions might be referred to it and it is possible that the oracle was bribed to answer in a certain way.

The most famous pronouncements were always ambiguous. In the Persian Wars the Athenians knew their city was under threat of destruction; they were advised to trust to their 'wooden walls'. This was variously interpreted to mean an ancient structure on the Acropolis, or the fleet (we shall come across this later – see Salamis in Chapter 5). A similar case arose in 546 BCE, and was in some ways the root cause of what we shall discuss in Chapter 4. King Croesus of Lydia, who was about to make war on Persia, was told that if he crossed the River Halys (the boundary) he would destroy a great empire. He did – it was his own empire that was overthrown by Cyrus the Great. Of course, you could say that the oracle was hedging its bets.

10 THINGS TO REMEMBER

1 Greek religion is different from later religions, which are usually monotheistic and have a clear code of belief.

2 Many gods were purely local in origin, and it was often the poets who fitted them into a larger structure.

3 There were regular ceremonies and sacrifices to keep the gods 'on our side'.

4 Olympia is an example of a sacred site. The Olympic Games were designed to honour Zeus.

5 Myths are stories that explain how the worlds of gods and humans were related.

6 There were twelve Olympian gods, but also many minor deities.

7 Myths and legends tell us that Zeus and the Olympians had replaced an earlier generation of gods, who were known as the Titans.

8 Gods are amoral, and capricious in their behaviour.

9 One way of understanding the gods' wishes was by observing omens.

10 Oracles, established at sacred sites such as Delphi, were places where knowledge of the future might be obtained.

Early philosophy – Ionia

Aim

In this chapter we examine the role of the Ionian cities in early Greek thinking and science. At the end of the chapter you should be able to understand the background to the following question, while appreciating that it contains a modern view of the subject under discussion.

▶ How did mythological ways of thinking change to more rationalistic and scientific perceptions?

In terms of the general historical narrative you should also be able to understand and answer this question.

▶ How did the Ionian revolt trigger the first Persian War?

A guide to the pronunciation of important names in this chapter.

THALES (*th* as in 'health', not as in 'they'– *thaylees*; stress on the first syllable).

HERACLITUS (as written – long '*i*', which takes the stress).

LOGOS (stress on the first syllable). Greek for 'word'. It has further extended meanings – 'speech', 'language' and 'reason', which culminate in the religious use at the beginning of St John's Gospel.

PYTHAGORAS (*Pie-th* (as above) – short '*a*' takes the stress).

ERETRIA (stress on the second syllable). City on the island of Euboea.

HIPPIAS (*hippy-ass* with stress on the first syllable). Exiled tyrant of Athens used as a stooge by the Persians during their invasion.

Ionia

The focus of our investigations now shifts across the Aegean Sea to Ionia, which is the middle and southern portion of the western seaboard of what is now Turkey. Today the area is frequently visited on cruises or other Turkish holidays, and many Classical ruins are available for you to see, from Troy in the north to Izmir (where Old Smyrna, still being excavated, is a good example of an early Greek city). Further south you will find Ephesus, where the ruins cover an enormous area; this city survived for a long time and you may be interested to visit the theatre where St Paul was threatened by the silversmiths and the site of the house of the Virgin Mary in her old age. In Classical times Ephesus contained a huge temple to the goddess Artemis, but here she was presented as a mother-goddess rather than as a hunting and shooting young girl. It is possible that one can see the fusion of Greek with oriental ideas. Further south is Bodrum, called Halicarnassus by the Greeks, which is where Herodotus was born.

The intellectual awakening in Ionia

This area had been colonized and settled by the Greeks at an early period and Homer and Hesiod are thought to have come from there originally. Both of them, it might be said, in addition to the basic points made earlier, were not simple purveyors of religious truisms; both tried to make sense of the myths and stories, and their view of the gods was not uncritical.

The time of Ionian intellectual dominance began in the Archaic period, about 150 years later than these early poets. A succession of thinkers appeared who are usually referred to as the Pre-Socratics (i.e. they are the philosophers who come before Socrates). Their writings survive in a fragmentary state and information about them is sparse.

THE RISE OF SCIENTIFIC THINKING

We now need to consider and set against myth-making the first stages of what can be described as scientific thinking as an explanation of the world: words like 'scientific thinking' must be used carefully, but will serve in order to explain the direction in which the argument is moving.

Thales

The first of these thinkers is Thales, who came from the Ionian city of Miletus; he is reported to have predicted a solar eclipse in 585 BCE. Other stories credit him with mathematical skills of a high order, such as being able to work out the heights of the pyramids from the length of the shadows they threw. When he thought about the world, he announced the water was the *arche* (pronounced *are-key*), the beginning or first principle of all things; this is not quite the same as saying all things are made of water. Since there were only four elements, this was a quite a reasonable idea, especially as people believed from observations that living things were brought into being by the floods acting upon the mud of the river Nile.

His followers

Other philosophers arose with similar or parallel explanations of phenomena, utilizing the other elements of earth, fire and air in turn and all trying to establish that the world has unity, since unifying principles appeared to apply.

Insight

This idea – that there were, in essence, laws of Nature – was more important than the fact that the philosophers might contradict each other on what the unifying principle was, and certainly represents an advance on the mixed nature and oddity of mythological explanation.

Rather than survey all these philosophers, we have time to look at two extraordinary thinkers.

Heraclitus

Heraclitus, who was born in Ephesus and flourished c. 500 BCE, wrote in a cryptic style; we have inherited a series of obscure and fragmentary utterances, but it is now thought that they may always have been fragments. We forget that continuous prose was hardly in existence anyway. His thinking was also paradoxical, in that he interpreted phenomena in a way opposite to what you might expect. Below is an example.

The principle of Fire

▶ Heraclitus is usually alleged to have identified Fire as the main element in nature.
▶ But Fire, he argued, was only a vivid expression of *change*, which was really the first principle.

It is because things constantly move and change that they remain in existence. The problem is that some of Heraclitus's short and pithy sayings, which may have seemed anti-religious or highly rationalistic to his contemporaries, resound with other implications when translated into modern English. Although you might not expect it, his ideas have appealed to religious poets; see Gerard Manley Hopkins's sonnet on 'That Nature is a Heraclitean Fire…' and the epigraphs to T. S. Eliot's *Four Quartets*, which are quotations from Heraclitus: 'The way up and the way down is one and the same' and 'Though the word [logos] is common to all, most people live according to a private vision.' Among his other remarks the statement that 'The dry soul is wisest' might mean at its highest that the soul is best when it approaches the nature of the divine Fire; it is comforting to note that it also means that one should avoid alcohol and other forms of self-indulgence. In spite of his rationalizing tendencies his philosophy found room for 'the soul' as a dynamic force within the human being; in this some people have seen connections with Eastern religions.

Pythagoras

The link with Eastern religions is definitely true of Pythagoras's beliefs. In his case the likelihood that there may be some connection with Eastern religions is borne out by stories of his reputed travels in the East. Pythagoras came from Samos and was probably born c. 550 BCE. He moved to Croton, in what is now Southern Italy, and founded a kind of secret society. His writings have not survived. Nevertheless we know from later accounts that he was interested in mathematics and the famous theorem that bears his name comes out of these studies. The Pythagoreans were interested in *number* and theories of number as the clue to understanding the universe, but they are also famous for their religious precepts. Of these, the principal ideas were a belief in the after-life and, in particular, the theory of the transmigration of souls which could pass into other animals and other living creatures; this led to vegetarianism and presumably would have excluded the Pythagoreans from the rites of animal sacrifice that proliferated in traditional Greek religion.

While you have been offered only scanty information here, what do you make of these philosophers and their teachings in general?

Answer

It would seem that while their initial rational and scientific approach must have seemed like an attack on religious belief, the later members of the school felt the need to provide some kind of substitute for the religion they had ousted. Pythagoras taught a way of life.

The Ionian revolt

You may have noticed that some of the Ionian philosophers of the sixth century moved far away from their homeland, and taught in areas as distant as southern Italy. While this may simply have been the need to find a congenial environment for their teaching, they may also have felt the need to move for political reasons. The Greek cities of Ionia had always clung to the fringes of Anatolia (Turkey) and left the hinterland to be ruled by local kings, who were in their turn subject to successive empires. From 546 BCE, following the conquests of Cyrus the Great, these cities came under the control of the Persian Empire and seem, at first, to have paid their tribute and co-operated with the satraps or local governors without anxiety. It must be stressed that the Ancient World was full of these rather loose arrangements; provided you acknowledged who was ultimately master you were left to your own devices. But under the rule of the Persian king, Darius I, the impositions of the foreign government became more and more oppressive, and the favoured regimes in the cities were tyrannies. In 499 BCE the Ionian cities deposed some of these local tyrants and then revolted against the Persians. In their campaigns they were helped by two cities of the Greek mainland, Athens and Eretria. After six years the Persians managed to overturn the revolt by sheer weight of numbers and proceeded to reconquer their territory.

They then remembered who had assisted the Ionians. A fleet was prepared which sailed through the Aegean islands, recalling the inhabitants to their supposed allegiance; this was also an excuse for exacting tribute and demanding men for the battle. Having arrived at Eretria (on Euboea), the first city to be punished, they soon took the town.

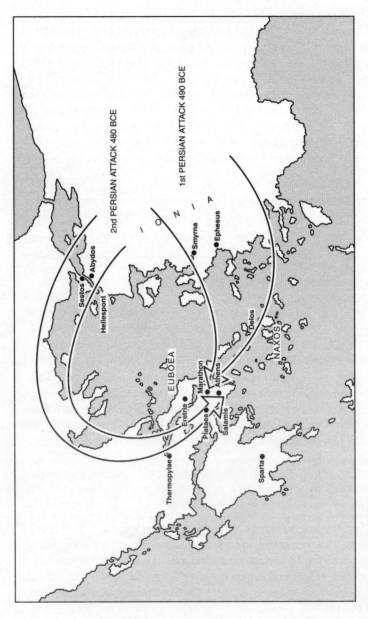

Figure 4.1 The Persian Wars

THE BATTLE OF MARATHON, 490 BCE

The Persians were led by Hippias, the exiled tyrant of Athens, to Attica and to the plain of Marathon where their cavalry could be deployed. They waited for the Athenians to support Hippias, but nothing of the kind happened. Athens was now a democracy and had no wish to reinstate him. In fact, the Athenians had assembled their army in the vicinity and were aided by their allies the Plataeans. They had approximately 10,000 men in all, the Persians had twice as many; so the Athenians resolved to wait for help from the Spartans, but this could not be sent as the Spartans were observing a festival. Eventually, the Athenians were persuaded by one of their generals, Miltiades, to attack the Persians, as it was reported that they were planning to move to Athens in their ships. They charged upon them and after a long battle the enemy was defeated and fled. As Herodotus reports: 'In the Battle of Marathon some 6,400 Persians were killed: the losses of the Athenians were 192.' The Persian plan to attack Athens by sea did not succeed as the Athenians made their way back to their city in two days. The Persian fleet returned across the Aegean.

10 THINGS TO REMEMBER

1 In those days Ionia (now in Turkey) was as Greek as mainland Greece and the islands.

2 Many famous poets, philosophers and the historian Herodotus were Ionian by birth.

3 Intellectually the early philosophers were ahead of their time. They began to think and argue in a scientific way.

4 Thales thought that water was the first principle.

5 Heraclitus thought that the first principle was fire, which in itself was an expression of change.

6 We only have short prose statements from these early philosophers.

7 Pythagoras, who left no writings, seems to have developed a new religion, involving the transmigration of souls.

8 The Persians upset the status quo in Ionia, and their taxation and other exactions led to the Ionian Revolt.

9 This led to a war with the Greeks, known as the First Persian War.

10 The Athenians and their allies defeated the Persians at the battle of Marathon in 490 BCE.

5

....

The fifth century – Sparta

Aim

At the end of this chapter you should be able to answer these questions.

▶ What were the main features of the Spartan system?
▶ What happened in the second Persian War?
▶ What happened at the Battle of Thermopylae?

These are the important Greek names encountered in this chapter with a note on their pronunciation.

LAKONIA (*lack-own-ee-a* with the stress on '*on*'). The name of the district in which Sparta is situated, to be found in the south-east of the Peloponnese.

LACEDAIMONIAN (*lass-ed-eye-mown-i-an* with the stress on '*mon*'). An alternative name for a Spartan.

THERMOPYLAE (*therm-o-pill-ee* with the stress on the second syllable). Greek for 'the hot gates', a narrow place on the road near Lamia, north of Athens.

DEMARATUS (*dem-uh-rah-tus* with the stress on the third syllable). The exiled king of Sparta who accompanied Xerxes as a consultant.

LEONIDAS (*le-on-i-das* with the stress on the second syllable). The King of Sparta who died at Thermopylae.

The site of Sparta

If you take an archaeological tour of the Peloponnese as part of your Greek holiday, you may well pass through Sparte, as Sparta is now called. Unfortunately, there is little to see there in the way of remains from the Classical past, unless you make an effort and hunt about, so that Sparta is often omitted from tourists' itineraries, or used as a lunch-stop on the way to Mistra (see Chapter 9). In fact, there probably never was much of architectural interest because the Spartans in historical times were not given to constructing monuments. For example, there was no fortification wall at all in Classical times because of the confidence of the people in their military system (explained below). Some people have dismissed the Spartan capital even in its heyday as 'a collection of villages'.

EARLY HISTORY OF SPARTA

Traditionally, the Spartans were thought to be the most active group of the Dorian invaders who had reached Greece in the Dark Ages c.1000 BCE. Their society was, for the sake of a word, normal, until they began to expand into the rest of the Peloponnese. In the eighth century they conquered their western neighbours, the Messenians, who were the inheritors of the district associated with ancient Pylos. The conquered people were employed to undertake all the servile tasks and were referred to as the Helots. In the seventh century there was a second war with the Messenians, and in order to suppress any chance of further revolt, the Spartans had to organize themselves into a military society, dedicated to keeping supremacy at home, and to dominating the surrounding area. Although they were able to wage war at a distance, it is worth noting that they never really controlled the entire Peloponnese. The Spartans campaigned vigorously abroad for freedom and were against tyranny; but, in general, they supported oligarchical states.

THE SPARTAN SYSTEM

Sparta was ruled by the Spartans (i.e. the military class), who were not allowed to take part in agriculture or business activities. The money they used was so archaic – it consisted of iron bars – that the ruling class probably never handled it and was provided with food and other necessities in a communal system. The education of the ruling class was a particularly severe form of character training, which has never really been emulated, even in English boarding schools. Sparta actually had *two* kings from different families (who ruled simultaneously), but they were a comparatively minor part of a peculiar system which included a citizen assembly and five ephors or magistrates. The ephors were elected annually and were never eligible for re-election. Their job was to enforce the constitution and they controlled the kings; two of them, for example, accompanied the kings in battle. Of course, the conquered earlier population – the Helots – were excluded from power.

The second Persian War

THERMOPYLAE AND SALAMIS

After the failure of Persia's expeditionary force to subdue its faraway province, Darius's successor Xerxes led the next attempt to assert control of Greece in 480–79 BCE. The size of his huge army and navy, estimated at the time to be 2,750,000 men, has probably been exaggerated. At first the Persians were successful, but this time the Greeks were united and prepared. After crossing the Hellespont the Persian army proceeded largely unhindered across northern Greece until the Spartans faced them at the narrowest place between the mountains and the sea, which is called Thermopylae (see Figure 4.1 at the end of Chapter 4); meanwhile, the Greek navy challenged the Persian fleet out at sea. Unfortunately, the Spartan position was impossible to hold indefinitely, because the knowledge of an outflanking route over a mountain pass was given to the Persians; the Spartans held out to the bitter end. At sea the naval action was inconclusive. After discussion of the cryptic advice from the Delphic oracle to trust their 'wooden walls' (see end of Chapter 3) it was resolved to evacuate the city of Athens and face the Persians in a sea battle at Salamis. Here the Persians were so cramped in by the narrow channel that they were unable to make use of their superiority in numbers and were easily defeated. Xerxes withdrew to Asia leaving his army to harry Greece. Eventually this, too, was defeated at the Battle of Plataea.

Go tell the Spartans

A KEY PASSAGE IN THE HISTORIES *OF HERODOTUS*

The bravery of the Spartans at Thermopylae was never forgotten.

We know about the Persian Wars from Herodotus's book *The Histories*, although, of course, we must bear in mind that it is written from a pro-Greek point of view. On the other hand it is worth pointing out that Herodotus was pro-Athenian rather than Spartan in his sympathies. Below is an extract about the preparations for the Battle of Thermopylae. Xerxes, who must have assumed he could simply intimidate people by his superiority in numbers, is unable to understand why the Spartans and their allies are holding the narrow way against his army and sends a spy to investigate.

During the conference Xerxes sent a man on horseback to ascertain the strength of the Greek force and to observe what the troops were doing. He had heard before he left Thessaly that a small force was concentrated here, led by the Lacedaemonians under Leonidas of the house of Heracles. The Persian rider approached the camp and took a thorough survey of all he could see – which was not, however, the whole Greek army; for the men on the further side of the wall which, after its reconstruction, was now guarded, were out of sight. He did, none the less, carefully observe the troops who were stationed on the outside of the wall. At that moment these happened to be the Spartans, and some of them were stripped for exercise, while others were combing their hair. The Persian spy watched them in astonishment; nevertheless he made sure of their numbers, and of everything else he needed to know, as accurately as he could, and then rode quietly off. No one attempted to catch him or took the least notice of him.

Back in his own camp he told Xerxes what he had seen. Xerxes was bewildered; the truth, namely that the Spartans were preparing themselves to die and deal death with all their strength, was beyond his comprehension, and what they were doing seemed to him merely absurd. Accordingly he sent for Demaratus, the son of Ariston, who had come with the army, and questioned him about the spy's report, in the hope of finding out what the behaviour of the Spartans might mean. 'Once before,' Demaratus said, 'when we began our march against Greece, you heard me speak of these men. I told you then how I saw this enterprise would turn out, and you laughed at me.

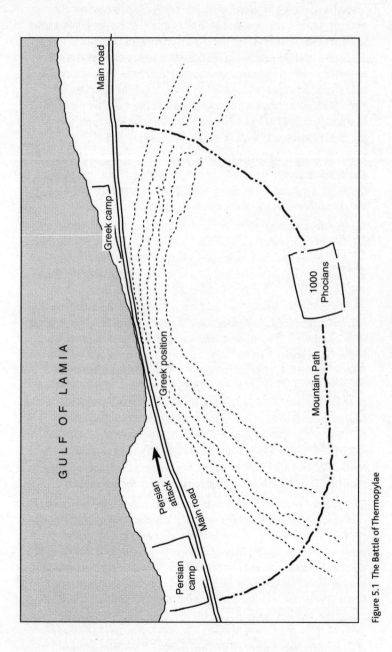

Figure 5.1 The Battle of Thermopylae

I strive for nothing, my lord, more earnestly than to observe the truth in your presence; so hear me once more. These men have come to fight us for possession of the pass, and for that struggle they are preparing. It is the custom of the Spartans to pay careful attention to their hair when they are about to risk their lives. But I assure you that if you can defeat these men and the rest of the Spartans who are still at home, there is no other people in the world who will dare to stand firm or lift a hand against you. You have now to deal with the finest kingdom in Greece, and with the bravest men.'

Xerxes, unable to believe what Demaratus said, asked further how it was possible that so small a force could fight with his army. 'My lord,' Demaratus replied, 'treat me as a liar, if what I have foretold does not take place.' But still Xerxes was unconvinced.

For four days Xerxes waited, in constant expectation that the Greeks would make good their escape; then, on the fifth, when still they had made no move and their continued presence seemed mere impudent and reckless folly, he was seized with rage and sent forward the Medes and Cissians with orders to take them alive and bring them into his presence. The Medes charged, and in the struggle that ensued many fell; but others took their places, and in spite of terrible losses refused to be beaten off. They made it plain enough to anyone, and not least to the king himself, that he had in his army many men, indeed, but few soldiers. All day the battle continued; the Medes, after their rough handling, were at length withdrawn and their place was taken by Hydarnes and his picked Persian troops – the King's Immortals – who advanced to the attack in full confidence of bringing the business to a quick and easy end. But, once engaged, they were no more successful than the Medes had been; all went as before, the two armies fighting in a confined space, the Persians using shorter spears than the Greeks and having no advantage from their numbers.

On the Spartan side it was a memorable fight; they were men who understood war pitted against an inexperienced enemy, and among the feints they employed was to turn their backs in a body and pretend to be retreating in confusion, whereupon the enemy would pursue them with a great clatter and roar; but the Spartans, just as the Persians were on them, would wheel and face them and inflict in the new struggle innumerable casualties. The Spartans had their losses too, but not many. At last the Persians, finding that their assaults upon the pass, whether by divisions or by any other way they could think of, were all useless, broke off the engagement *and withdrew. Xerxes was watching the battle from where he sat; and it is said that in the course of the attacks three times, in terror for his army, he leapt to his feet.*

Herodotus, *The Histories*, Book 7

Why do you think Herodotus told his story in this way?

Answer

This is a fairly typical piece of Herodotean narrative. Herodotus is concerned to preserve the records of 'human achievements so they may not be forgotten', and there is a sense in which history of this kind is a record of examples. I think it makes clear the kind of values that prevailed in the Spartan army, and also underlines the Greek view of the general idiocy of tyrants like Xerxes. The final sentence where he leaps to his feet gives us all we need to know about his character.

THE BATTLE

The rest of the story can be read in Herodotus Book 7. A number of points are made which add to the sense of doom or fate in the narrative. Leonidas dismissed all those who were unwilling to fight; he may have been inspired to commit himself to certain death in this way by an oracle from Delphi which said that either Sparta itself or one of its kings would die in the war.

THE EPITAPH

Herodotus tells us that he took the trouble to find out the names of all the 300 Spartans who died. Memorials were later placed in the pass. The most famous of these, by Simonides, said:

Take a message to the Spartans, passerby;
We carried out their orders; here we lie.

This can be translated more succinctly (and, therefore, laconically):

Go tell the Spartans, you who read,
We took their orders and are dead.

Insight

The sea has now retreated so the pass is not so easy to defend. In April 1941, during the Second World War, Australians and New Zealanders under General Freyberg found themselves at Thermopylae, preparing to fight a delaying action. The troops were only issued with five rounds of ammunition each, so this looked like another doomed battle. The Germans knew about the outflanking path from their Classics and could not have been held off for long. Before any fighting took place the Allied troops were ordered to retreat.

10 THINGS TO REMEMBER

1 Sparta is famous for the military organization of its society.

2 The Spartans were forced to adopt this method of government in order to keep the subject population of Helots in order.

3 The Second Persian War took place in 480–479 BCE.

4 The ruler of the Persians was Xerxes.

5 He brought an immense army across the Hellespont and into northern Greece.

6 At Thermopylae they were opposed by the Spartans, who were initially successful in holding the pass, though their army was very small.

7 The Spartans were betrayed, and were outflanked by the Persians who used a mountain path.

8 They fought to the end. It may be that this was not simply bravery. Leonidas was inspired to fulfil a Delphic oracle.

9 Though the Persians were able to capture the city of Athens, their navy was defeated at the Battle of Salamis.

10 Finally the Persian Army was defeated at the Battle of Plataea.

6

Imperialism and war – Athens

Aim

At the end of this chapter you should be able to answer some historical questions.

▶ What was the background to the rise of Athens in the first half of the fifth century?

▶ What were the aims of Athens and Sparta in this period?

▶ What happened to Socrates and why?

You should be able to discuss

▶ Some Athenian buildings in context, their features and the contrast between their present and former state.

These are the important Greek names encountered in this chapter with a note on their pronunciation.

AGORA (*agg-or-uh* with the stress on the first syllable). The market-place.

PARTHENON (*parth* (as in thick) *en-on* with the stress on the first syllable). Temple of the virgin goddess Athena.

ACROPOLIS (*uh-crop-o-liss* with the stress on the second syllable). Normally used of the central hill of Athens, a steep outcrop of rock which that was fortified in early times. The same word can be used of the citadel of other towns (e.g. Corinth).

ERECHTHEUM (*e-reck-thee-um* with '*th*' as in 'thin' and with the stress on the second syllable). The temple of Erechtheus, an early king of Athens.

CARYATIDS (*carry-at-ids* with the stress on '*at*'). Figures of women used instead of columns (e.g. on the porch of the Erechtheum).

SOCRATES (*soc-krat-eez* with the stress on the first syllable). Athenian philosopher.

PLATO (*play-toe* with the stress on the first syllable). Writer of philosophic dialogues.

THRASYMACHUS (*thra-sim-uh-kus* with the stress on the second syllable). Forceful character in *The Republic*.

THUCYDIDES (*thew-si-did-ease with stress on the second syllable*). Historian of the Pelopponesian War.

The history of Athens in the fifth century

EFFECT OF THE GREEK VICTORY IN THE PERSIAN WARS

It was not clear at the time just how decisive the victories of Salamis and Plataea were. After the departure of the Persians the Greeks could not be sure that that they would not return; and they remained a threat for many years. Because the Persians saw themselves as a superpower to whom all should pay tribute, they may simply have regarded their Greek expeditions as a moderately successful policing operation; the defeats they had suffered in Greece were in no way a challenge to their empire, and the main power-base of Persia remained intact.

Therefore, preparations for defence against another Persian attack were kept in place. Sparta must have looked like the obvious candidate for the military leadership of Greece, but the first actions of the Spartans after the Persian retreat seem to have been petty and small-minded. For example, the Persians had left the city of Athens in ruins, but the Spartans tried to prevent the Athenians from rebuilding its walls; however they were outwitted by Themistocles. Thereafter, they confined themselves to looking after their security at home; the Messenian helots (see Chapter 5) revolted after an earthquake in 464 BCE, and then the Spartans had further troubles in the north of the Peloponnese.

THE DELIAN LEAGUE

Instead, it was the Athenians who achieved the leadership by exploiting the idea that their city had been the mother-city from which the Ionian colonies had been founded (see Figure 1.1). These cities should form an alliance against the Persian threat; in this way Athens set up the Delian League to keep a naval force in being. This was provided for by the loan of ships from the larger nautical states and by the financial subscriptions of those allies who did not own fleets. At conferences on Delos each member city had one vote.

Insight

Delos was a small island centrally placed between Greece and Ionia. It was the birthplace of Apollo and Artemis, and was therefore sacred. It soon became a cult-centre for the Ionians.

This alliance was based on the islands and the cities surrounding the Aegean Sea, but caused suspicion among the other Greeks, especially those who adhered to different political structures (see Chapter 1). By the middle of the fifth century both Athens and Sparta had formed systems of alliances, Athens controlling what had become her empire by means of a naval force, while Sparta, which was firmly based in the Peloponnese, relied on its exceptional and seemingly unbeatable military strength.

What was the difference between the Athenian and the Spartan alliances?

Answer

While the Athenians were based on the islands of the Aegean the Spartans were concerned solely with guarding the land approaches to their central position in the Peloponnese. In fact, they did not control the whole of that area. However, their alliance with the sea power of Corinth extended their influence.

THE FIRST WAR BETWEEN THE ALLIANCES

The first Peloponnesian War was fought between Athens and Corinth c. 461–446 BCE with the Spartans and their allies occasionally taking part. But the Athenians, though mainly successful, began to overreach themselves. An attempt to relieve a Greek base in Egypt failed with considerable losses; and the treasury of the Delian League was removed from Delos to Athens (454 BCE). This was a purely temporary measure, of course – but the treasury remained at Athens. Nevertheless, the Athenians did not immediately use these resources to beautify their city as is commonly assumed; throughout most of the first half of the century the Acropolis remained a ruin.

THE ATHENIAN EMPIRE

When the Delian league turned into an Athenian Empire is a matter of dispute. Tribute rather than free payment became the order of the day and Athens began to use the fleet to control the allies and to prevent secession; Naxos and Thasos were both forced back into the league in the 460s. After 450 BCE, when the Persians made a formal peace, the reason for the existence of the league was called in question. But the Athenians now regarded these cities as unquestionably theirs and they continued to apply a harsh policy and punished any cities that tried to withdraw.

THE SECOND OR GREAT PELOPONNESIAN WAR (431–405 BCE)

The course of this war is too complex to outline in a short account such as this, but Athens kept her empire together almost until the end of hostilities. The course of the war involved both sides in attempts to seize territory. In the Aegean there were one or two islands which were friendly to Sparta; when the island of Melos was conquered by Athens an attempt was made to persuade the inhabitants to join the League.

THE MELIAN DEBATE (416 BCE)

Thucydides (c. 460–400 BCE), who is the historian of the Peloponnesian War, tried to be as accurate as possible in his account of events, but to enliven his text he wrote part of it in direct speech; since he was not at all the events he described nor were modern methods of recording speech available, he contrived to put into the text what the characters would have said. Here the Athenians are summing up in the debate:

Do not be led astray by a false sense of honour – a thing which often brings men to ruin when they are faced with an obvious danger that somehow affects their pride. For in many cases men have still been able to see the dangers ahead of them, but this thing called dishonour, this word, by its own force of seduction, has drawn them into a state where they have surrendered to an idea, while in fact they have fallen voluntarily into irrevocable disaster, in dishonour that is all the more dishonourable because it has come to them from their own folly rather than their misfortune. You, if you take the right view, will be careful to avoid this. You will see that there is nothing disgraceful in giving way to the greatest city in Hellas when she is offering you such reasonable terms – alliance on a tribute-paying basis and liberty to enjoy your own property. And, when you are allowed to choose between war and safety, you will not be so insensitively arrogant as to make the wrong choice. This is the safe rule – to stand up to one's equals, to behave with deference towards one's superiors, and to treat one's inferiors with moderation. Think it over again, then, when we have withdrawn from the meeting, and let this be a point that constantly recurs to your minds – that you are discussing the fate of your country, that you have only one country, and that its future for good or ill depends on this one single decision which you are going to make.

The Athenians then withdrew from the discussion. The Melians, left to themselves, reached a conclusion which was much the same as they had indicated in their previous replies. Their answer was as follows:

'Our decision, Athenians, is just the same as it was at first. We are not prepared to give up in a short moment the liberty which our city has enjoyed from its foundation for 700 years. We put our trust in the fortune that the gods will send and which has saved us up to now, and in the help of men – that is, of the Spartans; and so we shall try to save ourselves. But we invite you to allow us to be friends of yours and enemies to neither side, to make a treaty which shall be agreeable to both you and us, and so to leave our country.'

What are the main points in the debate?

Answer

The Athenians assert that their strength allows them to dictate terms to the Melians; they offer alliance and demand tribute. The Melians wish to retain their liberty and offer neutrality.

Later on, after the Melians continued to resist, the men were put to death and the women and children sold into slavery.

THE END OF THE WAR

In spite of the forceful nature of the Athenians which Thucydides reveals, they eventually lost the war, principally because the Spartans, in alliance with the Persians, were able to defeat the Athenian fleet and sever the supply route from the Black Sea. After the Peloponnesian War ended there was a brief period of Spartan supremacy. Athens was compelled to break down her long defensive walls and the city was ruled for a time by 30 appointees selected by the Spartans. It was the rule of an oligarchy, a period later referred to as the rule of the Thirty Tyrants. This was brief. By 403 BCE democracy had been restored, but the mood was one of reaction.

Socrates and Plato

THE TRIAL AND DEATH OF SOCRATES

It was at this time (399 BCE) that the philosopher Socrates, possibly because he had taken many aristocratic pupils in the past, was put on trial for impiety. The exact words of the charge have been preserved:

> **Socrates is guilty of not believing in the gods which the city believes in, but of introducing other and new divinities. Also, he corrupts the young. The penalty demanded is death.**

Insight

There is an element of playing off old scores in this. Socrates had become famous as a teacher. His method seems to have been to provoke his pupils or opponents into dialogue. He asked awkward questions and frequently pretended to agree with something in order to make his opponents go out on a limb; he would then allow them to fall into pits of their own making. Such methods are highly amusing but create enmities.

Although he could have escaped from Athens and gone into exile, Socrates accepted the penalty of execution and drank the hemlock. Unfortunately he left nothing in writing and his friends composed literary dialogues to illustrate his teachings. He also featured in a play by Aristophanes, but most people would say that his portrait there is a caricature.

PLATO

We have to assume that the essential ideas of Socrates are preserved in the works of Plato, but this, too, is a matter of dispute. Of Plato it may be said that the manner of his writing is so charming that all readers are at first persuaded that the ideas he endeavours to express are as charming as the style. He has also attracted attention because of the mystical quality of some of his teachings. His views about the immortality of the soul, for example, have been tied in with Christian or other beliefs; further, his stories of Atlantis have made him the ancestor of Utopian fiction.

The method of instruction used by Plato was the dialogue, and we may as well begin with the opening of *The Republic* as an example of the narrative by which this form of literature can be introduced.

I went down yesterday to the Piraeus with Glaucon, son of Ariston. I wanted to say a prayer to the goddess and also to see what they would make of the festival, as this was the first time they were holding it. I must say that I thought that the local contribution to the procession was splendid, though the Thracian contingent seemed to show up just as well. We had said our prayers and seen the show and were on our way back to town when Polemarchus, son of Cephalus, noticed us in the distance making our way home and sent his slave running on ahead to tell us to wait for him.

The slave caught hold of my coat and said: 'Polemarchus says you are to wait.'

I turned and asked where his master was.

'He's coming along behind you,' he said. 'Do wait.'

'We will,' said Glaucon, and soon afterwards Polemarchus came up; with him were Adeimantus, Glaucon's brother, Niceratus, son of Nicias, and others who had all apparently been to the procession.

'Socrates,' said Polemarchus, 'I believe you are starting off on your way back to town.'

'You are quite right,' I replied.

'Do you see how many of us there are?' he asked.

'I do.'

'Well, you will either have to get the better of us or stay here.'

'Oh, but there's another alternative,' said I. 'We might persuade you that you ought to let us go.'

'You can't persuade people who won't listen,' he replied.

'No,' said Glaucon, 'you certainly can't.'

'Well, you can assume we shan't listen.'

'And don't you know,' added Adeimantus, 'that there is going to be a torch race in the evening on horseback, in honour of the goddess?'

'On horseback?' said I; 'that's a novelty. Do you mean a relay race, in which they carry torches on horseback and hand them to each other?'

'Yes,' answered Polemarchus, 'and there's to be an all-night carnival as well, which will be worth seeing. We will go out after dinner and watch it; we shall meet a lot of young men there to talk to. So please do stay.'

To which Glaucon replied, 'It looks as if we shall have to.'

'Well, if you think so,' I said, 'stay we must.'

So we went to Polemarchus' house, where we found his brothers Lysias and Euthydemus, and besides them Thrasymachus of Chalcedon, Charmantides of Paeania and Cleitophon, son of Aristonymus. Polemarchus' father, Cephalus, was there too; a very old man he seemed to me, for it was a long time since I had seen him last. He was sitting garlanded on some sort of an easy chair, as he had just been sacrificing in the courtyard. There were some chairs standing round about, so we sat down beside him.

The company decide to debate the nature of justice. Further on is an example of a character, Thrasymachus, who believes that might is right.

While we had been talking Thrasymachus had often tried to interrupt, but had been prevented by those sitting near him, who wanted to hear the argument concluded; but when we paused and I asked my question, he was no longer able to keep quiet but gathered himself together and sprang on us like a wild beast, as if he wanted to tear us in pieces. Polemarchus and I were panic-stricken, as Thrasymachus burst out and said, 'What is all this nonsense, Socrates? Why do you go on in this childish way being so polite about each other's opinions? If you really want to know what justice is, stop asking questions and then playing to the gallery by refuting anyone who answers you. You know perfectly well that it's easier to ask questions than to answer them. Give us an answer yourself, and tell us what you think justice is. And don't tell me that it's duty, or expediency, or advantage, or profit, or interest. I won't put up with nonsense of that sort; give me a clear and precise definition.'

I was staggered by his attack and looked at him in dismay. If I had not seen him first I believe I should have been struck dumb; but I had noticed him when our argument first began to exasperate him, and so I managed to answer him, saying diffidently: 'Don't be hard on us, Thrasymachus. If we have made any mistake in our consideration of the argument, I assure you we have not done so on purpose. For if we were looking for gold, you can't suppose that we would willingly let mutual politeness hinder our search and prevent our finding it. Justice is much more valuable than gold, and you must not think we shall slacken our efforts to find it out of any idiotic deference to each other. I assure you we are doing our best. It's the ability that we lack, and clever chaps like you ought to be sorry for us and not get annoyed with us.'

Thrasymachus laughed sarcastically, and replied, 'There you go with your old affectation, Socrates. I knew it, and I told the others that you would never let yourself be questioned, but go on shamming ignorance and do anything rather than give a straight answer.'

'That's because you're so clever, Thrasymachus,' I replied, 'and you know it. You ask someone for a definition of twelve, and add "And I don't want to be told that it's twice six, or three times four, or six times two, or four times three; that sort of nonsense won't do." You know perfectly well that no one would answer you on those terms. He would reply "What do you mean, Thrasymachus; am I to give none of the answers you mention? If one of them happens to be true, do you want me to give a false one?" and how would you answer him?'

'That's not a fair parallel,' he replied.

'I don't see why not,' I said: 'but even if it is not, we shan't stop anyone else answering like that if he thinks it fair, whether we like it or not.'

'So I suppose that is what you are going to do,' he said; 'you're going to give one of the answers I barred.'

'I would not be surprised,' said I, 'if it seemed to me on reflection to be the right one.'

'What if I give you a quite different and far better reply about justice? What do you think should be your penalty then?'

'The proper penalty of ignorance, which is of course that those who don't know should learn from those who do; which is the course I propose.'

'You must have your joke,' said he, 'but you must pay the fee for learning as well.'

'I will when I have any cash.'

'The money's all right,' said Glaucon; 'we'll pay up for Socrates. So give us your answer, Thrasymachus.'

> *'I know,'he replied, 'so that Socrates can play his usual tricks, never giving his own views and when others give theirs criticizing and refuting them.'*
>
> *'But, my dear man, what am I to do?' I asked. 'I neither know nor profess to know anything about the subject, and even if I had I've been forbidden to say what I think by no mean antagonist. It is much more reasonable for you to say something, because you say you know, and really have something to say. Do please therefore do me a favour and give me an answer, and don't grudge your instruction to Glaucon and the others here.'*
>
> *Glaucon and the others backed up my request, and it was obvious that Thrasymachus was anxious to get the credit for the striking answer he thought he could give; but he went on pretending he wanted to win his point and make me reply. In the end, however, he gave in, remarking, 'So this is the wisdom of Socrates: he won't teach anyone anything, but goes around learning from others and is not even grateful.'*
>
> *To which I replied, 'It's quite true, Thrasymachus, to say I learn from others, but it's not true to say I show no gratitude. I am generous with my praise – the only return I can give, as I have no money. You'll see in a moment how ready I am to praise a good answer, for I'm sure the one you're going to give me will be good.'*
>
> *'Listen then,' he replied. 'I say that justice or right is simply what is in the interest of the stronger party.'*

This is a good example of the dialogue in action and shows how Socrates plays with an opponent. Thrasymachus is defeated and seen off; but one wonders what the Melians might have thought of all this.

Finally here is a short extract from further on in *The Republic* where Socrates (or Plato) is beginning to be more prescriptive. Socrates is describing an ideal state, where things are quite different from Athens.

They have been discussing the drama and the principal objections to it at this stage are:

▶ that the stories in plays are morally objectionable
▶ that acting or dramatic recitation is unsuitable training for the young because they are made to impersonate bad characters.

'So,' says Socrates

> *'if we are visited in our state by someone who has the skill to transform himself into all sorts of characters and represent all sorts of things, and he wants to show off himself and his poems to us, we shall treat him with all the reverence due to a priest and giver of rare pleasure, but shall tell him that he and his kind have no place in our city, their presence being forbidden by our code, and send him elsewhere, after anointing him with myrrh and crowning him with fillets of wool. For ourselves, we shall for our own good employ story-tellers and poets who are severe rather than amusing, who portray the style of the good man and in their works abide by the principles we laid down for them when we started out on this attempt to educate our military class.'*
>
> *'That undoubtedly is what we should do,' he said, 'if we have the choice.'*
>
> *'And I think,' said I, 'that that probably completes our survey of the literature and stories to be employed in our education. We have dealt both with subject-matter and with form.'*
>
> *'I agree,' he replied.*

Faced with this you may begin to wonder what kind of ideal state this Republic is to be. Surely something far more like Sparta than Athens? In Chapter 7 we shall look at what went on in the theatres.

Athens and its monuments

Whereas Athens began as one among many equal cities, today it is the capital of Greece, its population swollen to a gigantic size in comparison to that of the past. Today most of the air routes to Greece converge on Athens. It is, therefore, likely that a trip to Greece would include a visit to Athens, and often there is time to spare. You will find that in the centre of Athens you can wander around the excavated market-place area – the ancient Agora – and go up to the Acropolis, which seems at first to be a collection of ruins, but there is plenty to see if you persevere.

THE PRESENT APPEARANCE OF THE CITY

Comparatively little has survived above ground in Athens to show us what such cities were like. Even the most famous temple, the Parthenon, has suffered in war. But there are some pleasing smaller structures such as the choregic monument of Lysicrates and the Tower of the Winds and, of course, the columns of the temple of Olympian Zeus. It is often said that you will see better cities in Turkey, where, for example, the ruins of Ephesus stretch to the horizon, and better temples in Italy and Sicily. This is partly the result of the accidents of history and partly because the Greeks in the 'colonial' areas were richer.

THE FORMER APPEARANCE OF THE CITY

It is difficult for us to imagine the amount of art and sculpture that surrounded daily life in such a city, partly because it was normal to show wealth in public structures, and partly because of the omnipresent demands of religion in its most general sense. There were many gods and local deities and it was felt that failure to honour them appropriately would bring retribution. The journeys of Pausanias (see Guide-books to Greece in Chapter 10) in the second century CE reveal how packed the cities were with temples and memorials of all kinds; there was sculpture everywhere, even though the first Romans to conquer Greece may have made off with quantities of material. It is difficult for us to take in the fact that most of the sculptures, like the temples themselves, were painted in colour.

THE DESTRUCTION OF ATHENS

Pausanias's journeys, though made seemingly late in time, were undertaken before belief in the gods had been subverted by Christianity,

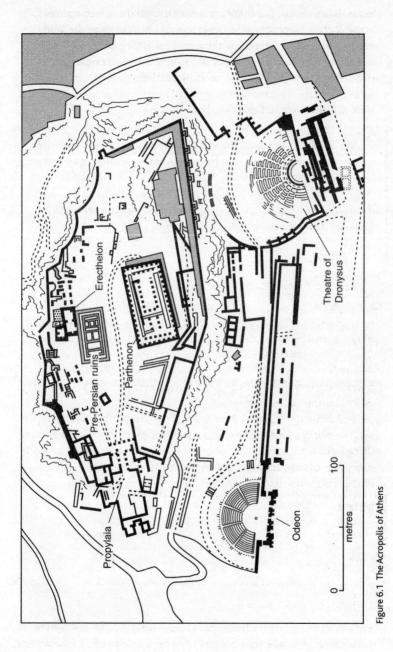

Figure 6.1 The Acropolis of Athens

Propylaia

Pre-Persian ruins

Erectheion

Parthenon

Odeon

Theatre of Dronysus

0

metres

100

so that the images were not yet open to destruction as idols, and they also took place before the systematic looting brought about by later invasions. For example, the Heruli, a barbarian tribe from outside the Roman Empire, raided Athens in 267 CE and it never really recovered; in the Middle Ages it declined into a village.

THE TEMPLES ON THE ACROPOLIS

As has been pointed out, the most complete examples of Greek temples have survived elsewhere, notably in Sicily and Italy, in the area that was known as Magna Graecia. In Athens itself the Parthenon, which has survived wars and the attentions of connoisseurs, now faces the ravages of pollution. Several other structures in Athens are in similar difficulties, for example, the Caryatids on the Erechtheum on the Acropolis have had to be replaced by copies.

THE PARTHENON

This temple is in the Doric style, and was erected in the second half of the fifth century from 447–433 BCE; the principal artist was Phidias, who is known to have made the colossal gold and ivory cult statue which was housed in the interior of the building. Because it attracted attention the Parthenon has had a sad history, although

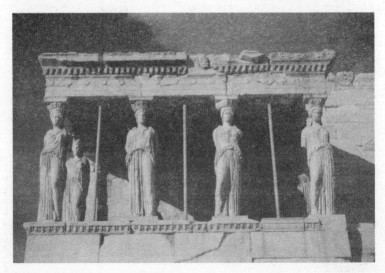

Figure 6.2 The Erechtheum with the Caryatids

the fact that it became a Christian church and a Moslem mosque may have helped its survival. However, most of its sculpture has gone and for quite different reasons. To see it you would have to return to London.

The Elgin marbles

The sculptures at the front, back and sides of the building – the pediments, the metopes and the frieze – were still in place in the seventeenth century when they were sketched by an artist; later an explosion took place within the structure. The sketches help us to reassemble the fragments which were removed by Lord Elgin in 1801–3 and were purchased by the British Government in 1816. They are now displayed in the British Museum in London, although the Greeks continue to challenge this theft of their heritage. The argument that the museum has looked after the sculpture well has also been challenged; we now know that the honey-coloured patina of the sculptures was scraped off early in the twentieth century so that the marble should appear white.

The subject of the frieze

Much of the sculptured frieze shows a procession. This has been identified as an interpretation of the Panathenaic procession which took place in August of each year; or, more exactly, of the great Panathenaic procession which took place every four years. A new robe of wool was prepared for the goddess but this was not taken to the Parthenon and the new image of ivory and gold; it went to the Erechtheum, where the ancient wooden image was kept.

But there are problems with this interpretation of the subject of the frieze. No other temple at that time would have had a sculpture depicting activities at the temple which it adorned. Therefore, it has been suggested that there may be some other meaning in the frieze. If you count the horsemen, of whom there seem to be an unnecessarily large number, the total comes to 192.

Insight

What does this remind you of? Revisit the Battle of Marathon description at the end of Chapter 4 if you don't remember.

Answer:

The figure 192 was, according to Herodotus, the number of the Athenian dead at the Battle of Marathon.

It is now worth putting together Herodotus's *Histories*, which asserted the value of the Athenian contribution to the defeat of Persia with the widespread feeling in fifth-century Athens that they alone had held back the Persian threat. You will recall that Leonidas did not achieve much in that direction. The Athenians continued to hold off the Persians with the Delian League. From all this, the commemoration of the Dead at Marathon seems an appropriate war memorial for a democratic state and a reminder of present reality.

The Erechtheum

The Erechtheum is a smaller temple on the Acropolis with quite a complicated history. Remember that this was where the cult statue of Athena was housed; from the main building extends a large porch – a good example of a structure with Ionic columns. Another feature is the smaller porch where columns have been replaced by figures of women. I'm afraid that these columns have, in turn, been replaced by facsimiles as the originals have been placed in a museum. One of these is in the British Museum.

What do you think these figures of women represent?

Answer

This is a puzzle at first because in these politically correct days you might want to think that the women represent – at last – a feminine contribution to the glory of Athens. According to Vitruvius the Roman architect, they represent the women of the town of Caryae, which had taken the side of the Persians – hence Caryatids. After the war the men were killed and the women were enslaved; here their punishment notionally continues as they are condemned to carry the weight of the roof for ever. However, it remains an artistic puzzle because everybody seems to admire the women, and such figures had been used elsewhere in Greece before this occasion.

Theatres

There are two theatres near the Acropolis, the Odeon which is a Roman structure and the theatre of Dionysus; the latter is the most important, as it takes us back – in imagination at any rate – to the beginnings of the drama.

The theatre of Dionysus

The original theatres for which the great plays were written may have been simple wooden structures with the audience sitting on earthen ramparts. The only scenery was probably a kind of mound in the centre of the acting area. The structure of the theatre of Dionysus now visible has been added to and adapted by Greeks and Romans since the plays of the great dramatists were first performed here. Later theatres incorporated a permanent backdrop of stone – the wall of the *skene* (scene) shaped like the outer aspect of a house with doors and other features, and we are not sure when the wall 'H–H'

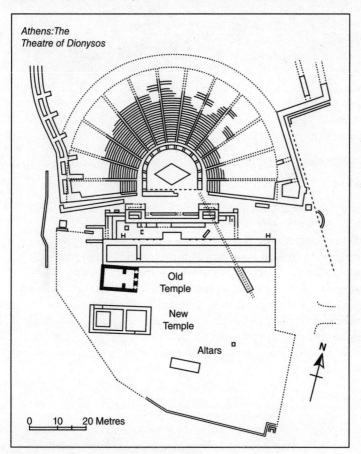

Athens: The
Theatre of Dionysos

Old
Temple

New
Temple

Altars

N

0   10   20 Metres

Figure 6.3 Plan of the theatre of Dionysus at Athens

on the diagram, which seems to be the base of this, was added. The roof of the skene may have been the base for a crane used for the splendid entrances of gods – the *deus ex machina*. In front of the skene was the orchestra or dancing place for the chorus. The seats were arranged in a semi-circle, and in this case you can see the front row has been adapted so that there are special seats for very important persons. All this will become clearer when the theatre at Epidaurus is discussed in Chapter 7.

10 THINGS TO REMEMBER

1 In the fifth century BCE Athens became the leading city in Greece.

2 This was achieved by setting up an alliance – The Delian League – that became an empire.

3 The Peloponnesian War between Athens and her allies and the Spartans and their allies lasted from 431 to 405 BCE.

4 Thucydides wrote the history of this war. It was not Athenian propaganda since the Melian debate shows Athens in a bad light.

5 Socrates was put to death for allegedly challenging the established religion.

6 After his death his ideas were expounded in the dialogues of Plato.

7 In Athens you can still see the Parthenon and other buildings from this period.

8 Lord Elgin took the Parthenon frieze to London in 1816.

9 The Erechtheum has a porch where the roof is held up by statues of women, called Caryatids.

10 Although it was subsequently modified, the theatre of Dionysus was the original home of Greek drama.

The fourth century – Epidaurus and its theatre

Aim

By the end of this chapter you should be able to answer these questions.

▶ What were the main features of dramatic festivals and early drama?
▶ What took place at a healing centre?

Here are the principal names encountered in this chapter with their pronunciation:

EPIDAURUS (*ep-pee-door-us* with the stress on the third syllable). Today it is known as Epidavros with the stress on the second syllable.

SOPHOCLES (*sof-o-klees* with the stress on the first syllable). The second important Greek dramatist, 496–406 BCE.

MENANDER (stress on the second syllable) c. 344–291 BCE. Comic writer.

ASCLEPIUS (*as-klee-pee-us* with stress on the second syllable). Hero who became the god of healing.

CLYTAEMNESTRA (*kli-tem-nees-tra* with the stress on the first and third syllables). The wife of Agamemnon.

At Epidavros (Epidaurus), to which tourists are usually taken on archaeological tours, a splendid fourth-century theatre survives with the seats almost intact. It is still used for performances and the acoustics are so good that you can hear the slightest sound at the back of the theatre even though it is in the open air. The reason that the theatre has survived is that it was sited in such a remote place.

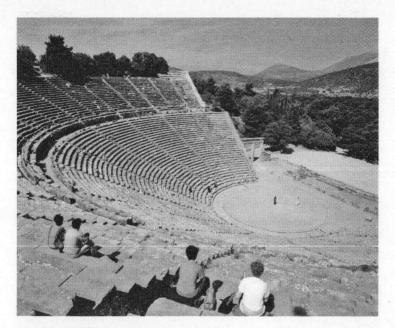

Figure 7.1 Epidaurus, the theatre, fourth century BCE

In Classical times it was included in a sacred precinct, where people went to have their illnesses treated by divine means; the theatre was part of a complex of buildings used for such healing.

Insight

In some ways this might be compared to Bath in eighteenth-century England, where people went to be cured by the waters but found the time to take part in all kinds of entertainment.

The drama

NATURE AND HISTORY OF GREEK THEATRE

From the earliest times, civic and communal life was expressed in festivals and ceremonies. The drama was presented at religious festivals, which most of the citizens were able to attend; in Athens, playwrights submitted three tragedies and a satyr-play – a kind of comic dance – in honour of Dionysus, and competed for prizes in the theatre dedicated to the god (see Chapter 6). Rich sponsors put up the money for the productions. This became a great civic event, to which foreign ambassadors were invited. We normally read the play-texts in isolation and tend to forget the 'municipal' background to this kind of theatre.

Later, the more famous plays were presented outside the original location and may have been taken on tour by itinerant poets and actors. Presenting plays was an expensive business because it was necessary to pay for the training of the chorus. Finally, in Roman times, the theatrical experience may have been reduced to a series of declamations.

THE SUBJECT-MATTER OF THE DRAMA

The division between tragedy and comedy began early. Here we are concerned with tragedy. While there is one early play by Aeschylus that deals with contemporary affairs – *The Persians*, produced in 472 BCE – the stories behind most of the tragedies were from legendary times. Few of them were, therefore, set in Athens, where they were written, and the action of many of the plays was supposed to be happening at places like Troy or Thebes, which were the scenes of the legends. However, it is not at all clear how conscious the playwrights were of the historical setting (in the way in which today television producers aim to have, say, every aspect of a Jane Austen novel accurately rendered and reduced to its Regency background); they may have preferred the imaginative release of a situation far removed from the present place and time. For a start there was little or no scenery at first, and even though we now think that there was considerable development here, a realistic stage-setting was not possible or required. Although most of the stories in the plays had their origin in Homer or oral tradition, playwrights freely adapted the material and were able to create tension in the plays; by allowing the characters to drift unaware into tragic situations which the audience already knew would happen, they were able to exploit dramatic irony. The *Oedipus Rex* of Sophocles is a great example of this.

Insight

Oedipus Rex

Oedipus was the King of Thebes. In the play he discovers that he has killed his father and married his mother. As the audience know the story, they are fascinated to see how the leading character stumbles on his way towards finding out the truth.

THE CHORUS AND ITS FUNCTION

Furthermore, each play was accompanied by a chorus of singers, who were trained to dance in a measured way as they sang. Usually they had some notional part in the action; they were the townspeople or a group of visitors to the scene. They sang of shared values and warned the characters to avoid unsocial behaviour. Sometimes one gets impatient with the triteness of some of the choric odes; nevertheless, these were an important part of the inherited structure and, in bringing out the morality behind the plays, they must have shown its relevance to contemporary life.

Here is a chorus from Sophocles's Antigone; *although it is related to the main text it also works as a free-standing poem. What is it about? Although the play is well known you may need to be told that Antigone has defied the laws of the city by burying her dead brother; when this chorus is sung nobody knows that she has done this.*

CHORUS:

                                  Numberless wonders
terrible wonders walk the world but not the match for man—
that great wonder crossing the heaving gray sea,
                    driven on by the blasts of winter
on through breakers crashing left and right,
    holds his steady course
and the oldest of the gods he wears away—
the Earth, the immortal, the inexhaustible—
as his plows go back and forth, year in, year out
    with his breed of stallions turning up the furrows.

And the blithe, lightheaded race of birds he snares,
the tribes of savage beasts, the life that swarms the depths—
                              with one fling of his nets
woven and coiled tight, he takes them all,
man the skilled, the brilliant!
He conquers all, taming with his techniques
the prey that roams the cliffs and wild lairs,
training the stallion, clamping the yoke across
    his shaggy neck, and the tireless mountain bull.
And speech and thought, quick as the wind
and the mood and mind for law that rules the city—
    all these he has taught himself

and shelter from the arrows of the frost
when there's rough lodging under the cold clear sky
and the shafts of lashing rain—
　　　　ready, resourceful man!
　　　　　　Never without resources
never an impasse as he marches on the future—
only Death, from Death alone he will find no rescue
but from desperate plagues he has plotted his escapes.

Man the master, ingenious past all measure
past all dreams, the skills within his grasp—
　　he forges on, now to destruction
now again to greatness. When he weaves in
the laws of the land, and the justice of the gods
that binds his oaths together
　　　　he and his city rise high—
　　　　　　but the city casts out
that man who weds himself to inhumanity
thanks to reckless daring. Never share my hearth
never think my thoughts, whoever does such things.

Discussion

This will be quite hard for those of you unused to reading poems
of this length, and the translation, while trying to do justice
to the original, does seem to duck and weave about. To risk a
generalization, the Greeks were very interested in Man's capacities in
the Classical period and may be described as humanists in that they
see man, not the gods, as all-important. Here we are given examples
of man's power over Nature – the sea and the earth in verse 1; the
birds, the fish and the animals in verse 2; the use of language and
the skills of rearing cities and providing shelter in verse 3. But at the
end of this verse we realize that even the conquest of disease will not
prevent man becoming prey to death in the end. In the fourth verse
the chorus at last seems to take notice of the story of the play, where
an unknown person has defied the laws of the city; only by keeping
to such laws can we be safe. To defy them brings uncomfortable
thoughts to mind.

It must be pointed out that *Antigone* was written c. 441 BCE and was
first performed in Athens, not Epidaurus. But the fourth century saw
a decline in the writing of tragedy and plays like this would have been

revived and kept alive. I tried to choose a chorus which seemed to express the natural setting of this theatre.

A GREEK PLAY IN ACTION

The only way to appreciate the Greek theatre is to read the play-texts or better still to attend a performance; the performances at Epidaurus are usually in Greek. It is quite amazing to think what great performances have taken place in the United Kingdom during the last 20 years. In the space available here we have time to look at an extract from the *Agamemnon* of Aeschylus. But first, the story of the play. This may seem to take away the tension, but the Greeks would have known the main points of the legend anyway.

The story of the Agamemnon

You will recall that Agamemnon was the legendary king of Mycenae at the time of the Trojan War. The scene is laid in Argos which is nearby; for practical purposes Argos had replaced Mycenae in historic times.

At the beginning of the play, we meet a watchman who is lying on the roof of a watchtower waiting for the sight of the beacon-fire which will announce the return of the king and his army. It is ten years since the armies left for Troy and there is still a hidden agenda to be enacted. On the way to Troy the fleet had been delayed by contrary winds and Agamemnon had sacrificed his daughter Iphigeneia. As a result he has alienated the affections of his wife Clytaemnestra. She has taken a lover, Aegisthus, and the two of them rule in Argos.

When Agamemnon finally arrives he is accompanied by Cassandra, a former princess of Troy, who is part of his loot. She has the gift of prophecy together with the contrary disadvantage that no one will understand her. Agamemnon enters his palace and both he and Cassandra are murdered by Clytaemnestra; he was in his bath and unable to resist. The chorus of townspeople are shocked but cannot intervene as they are the old men of the city. Aegisthus and Clytaemnestra announce that they will continue to rule as the play closes.

Comment and explanation

This is only the first play of a trilogy in which order is eventually restored. Agamemnon's son Orestes will one day grow to maturity and will attempt to return things to their proper place. He murders his mother, an unthinkable deed that is the equivalent of breaking a taboo; this will unleash the Eumenides, the Furies, who will haunt him until he is released from them at the end of the third play. Although Clytaemnestra is traditionally played as the villainess, one must comment upon the clash of male and female values; second, upon the great parts for women that this play affords; and third, it must be made clear that there is no particular sympathy for Agamemnon, who is portrayed as a foolish military man.

The task of the dramatist
Remember that the audience knew the rough outline of the story as well as we might be familiar with stories of King David or other heroes. But the treatment of the story and its events is brought up to date. For example, the human sacrifice, which initiated the drama ten years previously, may have been acceptable in the Bronze Age, but it is not to be admired or excused in the fifth century when the play was written. Aeschylus is a harsh moralist and understands how Clytaemnestra feels the right to exact personal vengeance, even though murder is as bad as the sacrifice. This kind of tension between two kinds of right is necessary to make drama and, on top of this, special effects are used to make interesting what is already foreseen. In the extract below, from the middle of the play, Clytaemnestra welcomes the king who has arrived in his chariot and is, of course, quite unaware of her plans for him.

CLYTAEMNESTRA:
        Come to me now, my dearest,
down from the car of war, but never set the foot
that stamped out Troy on earth again, my great one.
Women, why delay? You have your orders.
Pave his way with tapestries.   900

> *They begin to spread the crimson*
> *tapestries between the king and*
> *the palace doors.*

        Quickly.
Let the red stream flow and bear him home
to the home he never hoped to see – Justice,
lead him in!
        Leave all the rest to me.
The spirit within me never yields to sleep.   905
We will set things right, with the god's help.
We will do whatever Fate requires.

AGAMEMNON:
There
is Leda's daughter, the keeper of my house,
And the speech to suit my absence, much too long.
But the praise that does us justice,   910
let it come from others, then we prize it.
This –
you treat me like a woman. Grovelling, gaping up at me –
what am I, some barbarian peacocking out of Asia?
Never cross my path with robes and draw the lightning.
Never – only the gods deserve the pomps of honour   915
and the stiff brocades of fame. To walk on them ...
I am human, and it makes my pulses stir
with dread.
Give me the tributes of a man
and not a god, a little earth to walk on,
not this gorgeous work.   920
There is no need to sound my reputation.
I have a sense of right and wrong, what's more –
heaven's proudest gift. Call no man blest
until he ends his life in peace, fulfilled.
If I can live by what I say, I have no fear.   925

CLYTAEMNESTRA:
One thing more. Be true to your ideals and tell me –

AGAMEMNON:
True to my ideals? Once I violate them I am lost.

CLYTAEMNESTRA:
Would you have sworn this act to god in a time of terror?

AGAMEMNON:
Yes, if a prophet called for a last, drastic rite.

CLYTAEMNESTRA:
But Priam – can you see him if he had your success?   930

AGAMEMNON:
Striding on the tapestries of god, I see him now.

CLYTAEMNESTRA:
And *you* fear the reproach of common men?

AGAMEMNON:

The voice of the people – aye, they have enormous power.

CLYTAEMNESTRA:

Perhaps, but where's the glory without a little gall?

AGAMEMNON:

And where's the woman in all this lust for glory?   935

CLYTAEMNESTRA:

But the great victor – it becomes him to give way.

AGAMEMNON:

Victory in this … war of ours, it means so much to you?

CLYTAEMNESTRA:

O give way! The power is yours if you surrender all of your
own free will to me.

AGAMEMNON:

                                        Enough.

If you are so determined –   940
                        Turning to the women, pointing to
                        his boots.
Let someone help me off with these at least.
Old slaves, they'd stood me well.

                                        Hurry,
and while I tread his splendours dyed red in the sea,
may no god watch and strike me down with envy
from on high. So much shame I feel,   945
to tread the life of the house, a kingdom's worth
of silver in the weaving …

                                        And now,
since you have brought me down with your insistence,   955
just this once I enter my father's house,
trampling royal crimson as I go.
                        He takes his first steps and pauses.

CLYTAEMNESTRA:

                        There is the sea
and who will drain it dry? Precious as silver,
inexhaustible, ever-new, it breeds the more we reap it –

tides on tides of crimson dye our robes blood-red.   960
Our lives are based on wealth, my king,
the gods have seen to that.
Destitution, our house has never heard the word.
I would have sworn to tread on legacies of robes,
at one command from an oracle, deplete the house –   965
suffer the worst to bring that dear life back!

> *Encouraged,* AGAMEMNON *strides to the entrance.*

When the root lives on, the new leaves come back,
spreading a dense shroud of shade across the house
to thwart the Dog Star's fury. So you return
to the father's hearth, you bring us warmth in winter   970
like the sun –

> And you are Zeus when Zeus
tramples the bitter virgin grape for new wine
and the welcome chill steals through the halls, at last
the master moves among the shadows of his house, fulfilled.

> AGAMEMNON *goes over the threshold;*
> *the women gather up the tapestries*
> *while* CLYTAEMNESTRA *prays.*

Zeus, Zeus, master of all fulfilment, now fulfil our prayers –975
speed our rites to their fulfilment once for all!

> *She enters the palace, the doors close,*
> *the old men huddle in terror.*

What are the points leading to tension in this scene?

a) between Agamemnon and his better nature?
b) between Clytaemnestra and Agamemnon?
c) between what Agamemnon knows and what the audience knows
   (because the audience is already aware of the main outline of the
   story: remember we call this 'dramatic irony')? (Just note the line
   references if you can.)

Answer

a) Line 911 onwards. Agamemnon is very conscious that Greeks
generally, and soldiers in particular, don't do this sort of thing. It
is barbarian, it is hubristic ('hubris' is a Greek word meaning to

challenge the gods with your excessive pride (lines 944–5)), for a
military leader to walk on carpets.

Besides it is unmanly, a giving in to women, really a point under b).
Finally, the giving up of his real self is somehow connected with
taking off his boots and ceasing to be a man and a soldier.

b) Line 902 'let the red stream flow'. He thinks it refers to the carpet only
but hidden is an obvious reference to 'your blood will flow'.

In lines 926–40 an apparently gentle duel 'of wills' is fought between
them, which Clytaemnestra wins – foreshadowing how she will win
when she kills him in the house.

Similarly 'we will set things right' (906). He sees this as her offering
some kind of reconciliation for past differences but she means that
justice for Iphigeneia's death is now to be exacted.

Justice for Iphigeneia is also hidden in line 966 which he thinks refers to
his life; also 972.

c) Line 898–9 He thinks she means now between the carriage and the
palace. We know he will die soon and will never tread the earth again.

Many of the points listed at b) could equally come here. Similar
references to death and the unexpurgated root of what we would call
'sin' are hidden in 966–7. Look finally at 975–6 – the rites of Zeus
normally demand a blood-sacrifice, and we – but not Agamemnon –
know what form that sacrifice will take.

Healing at Epidaurus

Whether the actual audience in this theatre watched Aeschylus is
likely but unprovable; it does not always follow that the Greeks
admired the same drama that we do. Certainly, at the end of the
fourth century the fashionable members of the audience would have
expected to see a comedy by the contemporary dramatist Menander
from whom Roman comedy and ultimately much of Shakespearean
and later comedy has descended.

ASCLEPIUS THE HEALING GOD

The original Asclepius may have been a human physician but, by this time, he had been installed in the pantheon as an assistant to Apollo. Some doctors called themselves the sons of Asclepius. In the early stories he raised men from the dead and, as this would upset the natural order, Zeus killed him with a thunderbolt. He was associated with the caduceus, the staff with the sacred snake, which still appears in some medical contexts. The popularity of this and similar religious cults which appealed to the individual will be explored in Chapter 8; it is evidence of a turning away from the official aspects of religion and a seeking out of personal access to the divine.

OTHER BUILDINGS ON THE SITE

A large area of this site has been excavated. It was a sacred area where nobody was allowed to be born and nobody was allowed to die. We can see evidence of buildings used as hostels – it was a long way from town, and they were needed for the process known as incubation. There was also a large number of what can only be described as health-farm and conference-centre structures: i.e. a gymnasium and a banqueting hall.

INCUBATION

After performing rites of purification the sick person would go to sleep in a special hall or dormitory; there would be an unusual bed, perhaps the hide of a sacrificed animal, and the person would wear a white robe. All jewellery, belts and constricting garments would be removed. During the night the god would communicate with the patients through dreams; it was important to remember these exactly. Sometimes the god would appear himself with assistants and perform cures.

COMMENT

The test of all this must have been that it worked and that patients were cured, either by miracle or by the time-honoured medical practice of letting the body recover by itself. By suggestion and auto-suggestion the human was brought into contact with the divine and healing was possible. The resemblance to the traditional hospital practice of Victorian England with long wards, darkened rooms, special clothing and teams of 'gods' walking the wards gives one cause for thought.

10 THINGS TO REMEMBER

1 At Epidaurus there is one of the best-preserved Greek theatres.

2 Epidaurus was a remote place, used as a sacred centre of healing.

3 Greek tragedy usually takes its stories from Homer or oral tradition.

4 These stories were already known to the audience.

5 Every play included a chorus. The singing and dancing either illuminated or contrasted with the sentiments expressed by the actors.

6 Dramatic irony means the exploitation of the actor's ignorance of the situation he/she is in. The audience is aware of the real situation.

7 The god of healing was Asclepius.

8 People were healed by incubation, that is to say they went to sleep in special halls.

9 There the god would communicate with the patient.

10 This is also an example of a special cult providing direct access to the god.

Hellenistic civilization – Alexandria

Aim

By the end of this chapter you should be able to answer the following questions in outline.

▶ What political and cultural changes occurred after 300 BCE as a result of Alexander's conquests?

▶ Is there any evidence of changes in religious belief?

Here are the important names in this chapter and their pronunciation:

BOEOTIA (*bee-oh-sha*). District north of Athens (also known after its capital – Thebes).

EPAMINONDAS (as written with the short syllables; the stress is on the fourth syllable). Theban general, died at Mantinea.

PTOLEMY (*toll-em-mee* with the stress on the first syllable). Ptolemy I was one of Alexander's generals who took over Egypt; from 304 BCE he and his descendants became a new Egyptian Pharaonic dynasty – the Ptolemies.

LAOCOON (*lay-ok-koh-on*; four syllables, with the stress on the second). Name of a statue of a Trojan priest who was involved in a struggle with a huge snake.

CALLIMACHUS (*cal-im-a-kus* with stress on the second syllable). Librarian and poet; most of his work was done in the reign of Ptolemy II 285–246 BCE.

THEOCRITUS (*thee-o-cri-tus* with the stress on the second syllable). Pastoral poet who flourished at the same time as Callimachus and lived c. 310–250 BCE.

Alexander and his successors

During the fourth century, sporadic warring continued in Greece; eventually Boeotia, long thought of as the dullest of the Greek states, took the supremacy from Sparta. Its army was led by a brilliant general, Epaminondas, who invented new tactics for dealing with the Spartan phalanx. But both Sparta and Thebes were exhausted by the struggle and their wars ended at the drawn Battle of Mantineia (362). Thereafter, the comparative weakness of the various Greek states made them open to threats of absorption from the powerful King Philip of Macedon, who eventually defeated the Greeks at the decisive Battle of Chaeroneia (338). His son Alexander, who began his rule in 336, was soon campaigning in Asia and Egypt. By 330 the Persian king Darius was dead and Alexander, claiming to have succeeded him, rapidly annexed the rest of the Persian Empire and moved to its eastern reaches. From there he pushed on into what is now Afghanistan and Pakistan. Everywhere he went he founded new Greek cities, usually called 'Alexandria', as the most famous one in Egypt is to this day. When he died in 323 he was in control of a vast empire (Figure 8.1).

A HELLENIZED WORLD

From this point the Hellenistic period may be said to begin, that is to say the time in which the rest of the known world was Hellenized, or became Greek – in the sense that the Greek language was adopted as the official language of the new states, and Greek fashions in dress and art prevailed. This influence was considerably deeper than mere externals, at any rate. What is amazing is that in spite of the rapidity of the conquest, much of the extended area conquered by Alexander remained Greek in language and culture for centuries, whatever political events took place. Alexander's generals inherited the empire but it soon fell apart. The successor states were Macedonia, which controlled Greece, Egypt under the Ptolemies, which at times took over much of the Eastern Mediterranean, and the kingdom of the Seleucid dynasty, which inherited most of the old Persian empire. In spite of rivalries and periodic frontier wars these areas remained largely Greek in culture until the arrival of the Romans in the first century BCE. Though this is the official end of the Hellenistic phase, reality was quite different. In many of these areas the Romans may

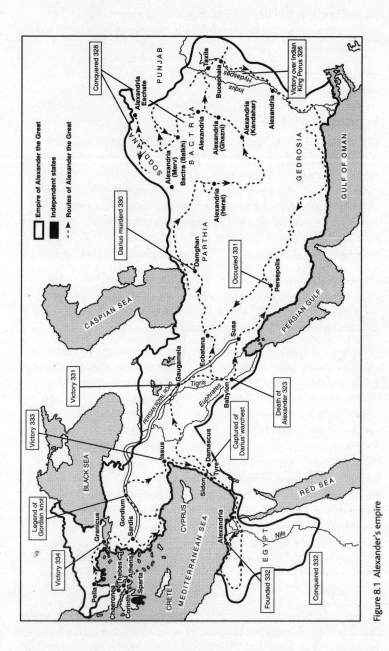

Legend:
- Empire of Alexander the Great
- Independent states
- ➤ Routes of Alexander the Great

Victory 334 — Pella · Chaeronea · Granicus · Thebes · Corinth · Athens · Sparta · Sardis · Gordium

Legend of Gordian knot

Victory 333

Victory 331

Darius murdered 330

Conquered 328 — PUNJAB · Taxila · Bucephala · Alexandria Eschate

Victory over Indian King Porus 326

SOGDIANA · Alexandria (Merv) · Bactra (Balkh) · BACTRIA · Alexandria · Alexandria (Ghazni) · Alexandria (Kandahar) · Alexandria · GEDROSIA · Hydaspes · Indus · GULF OF OMAN

Occupied 331 — Persepolis

Alexandria (Herat) · PARTHIA · Damghan · Ecbatana · Susa

CASPIAN SEA · Gaugamela · PERSIAN ROYAL ROAD · Tigris · Euphrates · Babylon · PERSIAN GULF

Captured of Darius' warchest

Death of Alexander 323

Victory 333 — BLACK SEA

Issus · Damascus · Tyre · Sidon

CYPRUS · MEDITERRANEAN SEA · CRETE

Alexandria · Founded 332 · EGYPT · Nile · Conquered 332 · RED SEA

Figure 8.1 Alexander's empire

have established military control, but everyday life remained as before and commercial and other transactions were still conducted in the Greek language.

Hellenistic culture

CONSOLIDATION

The acceptance of the new scheme of things was not immediate but in effect there was a long period of peace. Resources were available to beautify the cities and to set in order and codify the inheritance from the Classical period. The new cities flourished; even in India sculptors adopted and adapted Greek traditions. All over the area now enclosed within the Greek perimeter could be found cities with gymnasia and theatres. In spite of dynastic and other rivalries the new rulers soon felt stable enough to believe they had a right to be there.

Two buildings that date from this time, the Pharos at Alexandria and the Mausoleum at Mausolus (Bodrum), were often referred to as 'wonders of the world'. Though they have been destroyed, they are still remembered for their magnificence.

What is most noticeable about these structures, compared to the ideals of earlier generations of Greeks, is their sheer size. The Pharos was a useful building and needed to be tall so that its light could be seen far out at sea. The Mausoleum was an unnecessarily large tomb. These structures seem to show hubris and to go against the earlier axioms of 'Nothing too much' or 'Moderation in all things'. They also exemplify the rule of tyrants or god-kings as they were beginning to be referred to, and because of this seem to lose the humanistic ideals of previous generations. Alexander had wished for divine honours in order to consolidate his position in Persia and his successors in Egypt, the Ptolemies, took over the divinity of the Pharaohs. Also, one might observe, in the light of modern economic theories, that the designing and building of such vast architectural enterprises must, for a time, have provided considerable employment, not least to builders and the craftsmen and artists needed to decorate the structure.

In terms of our own cultural history, however, you must understand that it was for a long time the practice in teaching this period to regard its art as decadent. The example most often referred to in

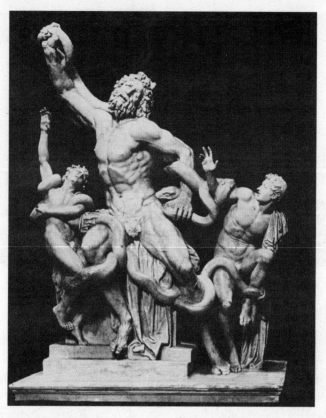

Figure 8.2 Laocoon: Vatican museum. The statue shows a Trojan priest and his two sons being attacked by a sea-serpent

support of this is the sculpture in Figure 8.2 with its writhing and pained figures. The Romans thought that the Laocoon was the height of Greek sculpture, which tells us a lot about Roman taste.

Egypt

A NEW AESTHETIC

In Egypt several influences came together, fused and then generated a new kind of culture, based upon the Greek technical skills but quite original. Figure 8.3, for example, shows structures from Egypt at

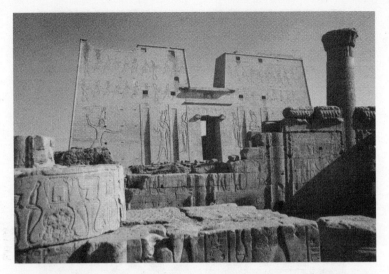

Figure 8.3 The temple at Edfu, built in the reign of the Ptolemaic kings, combines Greek and Egyptian influences

this time that have really only recently received due attention, being previously dismissed as a debased version of Egyptian art.

Of course, you can say that structures like these were simply built for show to advertise the power of the rulers, and were also designed to please the powerful Egyptian priesthood. After all, to the priests the Greek rulers were simply a new Egyptian dynasty. You could also say that the Greeks were living as a minority in a fixed cultural system and needed to overawe the mass of the Egyptian population. In fact, they had a good military basis and were the last of the Hellenistic kingdoms to submit to Roman rule.

ALEXANDRIA

Alexandria itself was different in that it was not meant to be a composite of Greek and Egyptian influences. It was founded as the new capital and was designed as a Greek city. From the air today you can still make out the original grid-plan. Because of earthquakes and subsidence much has been lost, but recently structures have been found submerged in the present harbour that seem to be part of the Greek city. In fact, placed where it was at the meeting of Asia,

Africa and Europe – for at that time Egypt controlled Cyprus and other Greek islands and cities – it became a world city. Its rulers sent out exploratory expeditions to the south and east. Scientific studies flourished: knowledge of the world increased, but there was also a curiosity about what had gone before.

The library at Alexandria

In this spirit the world-famous library was founded by Ptolemy II. Scrolls were gathered in from many sources and scholars were employed to set the texts in order. Editions of major Greek authors were undertaken. Ptolemy employed the priest Manethon to write a history of Egypt from the earliest times. Jewish scholars came from Jerusalem and were set to produce a Greek translation of the Pentateuch.

••

Insight

Pentateuch is the Greek name for the first five books of the Hebrew Bible.

••

CALLIMACHUS

All this scholarship in its turn generated new kinds of literature and, incidentally, employment for poets. Callimachus, who was a court-poet under Ptolemy II and III, wrote more than 800 books including a catalogue of the library; another prose-work was entitled 'Tables of those who have distinguished themselves in every form of Culture and of What they wrote'. Although only a few poems have survived, we can see that he was a typical scholar-poet of the new age. He perfected a new kind of witty poetry – alluding all the time to work of the past, whether directly or ironically. One of his poems is well known in this nineteenth-century translation. The 'nightingales' are assumed to be an allusion to the dead man's poetry. (The circumflex accent ^ means a long syllable.)

Hêraclîtus

> They told me, Hêraclîtus, they told me you were dead;
> They brought me bitter news to hear and bitter tears to shed.
> I wept, as I remember'd, how often you and I
> Had tired the sun with talking and sent him down the sky.
>
> And now that thou are lying, my dear old Carian guest,
> A handful of grey ashes, long, long ago at rest,
> Still are thy pleasant voices, thy nightingales, awake,
> For Death, he taketh all away, but them he cannot take.

WILLIAM CORY (*Epigr.* ii)

Do you have any literary comment to make?

Discussion

Words like 'charming' spring to mind; possibly it verges on the sentimental. In English this has become an anthology piece and this is appropriate because the Alexandrians were great compilers of anthologies. The level of emotion in the poem is also of its time; the Alexandrians turned out many charming little poems and epitaphs which sigh gently over the grave. What they don't seem to have – generalizing rashly – is a passionate engagement with life, and to some people they represent what literature in an unfree society has to descend to. Callimachus defended his limited kind of poetry on many occasions, saying that he valued 'a small drop from the pure spring' and that 'slim' poetry is of more interest than 'thick', which may be the clue to his work. Unfortunately, much of it is lost.

NEW FORMS OF LITERATURE

The detachment from the concerns of life 'as it is lived' led to the creation of a kind of substitute world in which, at any rate, some kind of passion could be expressed yet cause no offence. One result of this was the beginning of pastoral or bucolic poetry, the joys and sorrows of idealized shepherds, goatherds and their womenfolk living in a rural paradise. Their fields are full of love and song; all shepherds are poets, it seems. The inventor of this new world seems to have been Theocritus; (we shall look at an example from his work shortly, though of a different kind).

Insight

The pastorals were imitated by Virgil in his *Eclogues* and so came into the mainstream of later European poetry and general culture. Why else did Milton lament the death of Lycidas? Why else did Marie Antoinette play at being a shepherdess?

These new concerns led to parallel developments in prose; it is possible to say that in this culture we find the first romantic 'novels'.

Religion in the Hellenistic period

NEW DEITIES

The Greeks had always welcomed new gods and goddesses; the problem with Socrates was more fundamental than the charge brought against him indicated. For many years they had known of Oriental and Egyptian deities, giving them other names. Being now resident in Egypt, the Alexandrians were attracted by the teachings of the priests about the world beyond the grave, and their magical ceremonies; the cult of Isis, for example, who was able to restore her husband Osiris to life, attracted much attention. Because she brought fertility to the land she was identified with Demeter, and her cult was in some ways 'cleaned up' from the Egyptian original.

Adonis

Adonis was a young man beloved by Aphrodite (Venus, in Latin) who went hunting and was gored to death; his story has been celebrated by Shakespeare in *Venus and Adonis*. Every year the festival of Adonis was celebrated at Byblos (in the Lebanon) and also at Athens and Alexandria. This is where Theocritus can help us. The scene is Alexandria in the 270s BCE.

The characters in the urban 'pastoral' are as follows:

GORGO PRAXINOA	Women of Alexandria. They have a pronounced accent, which might be played as 'Estuary' English.
FIRST MAN SECOND MAN	Men who belong to the crowd.

Non-speaking parts are:

EUNOA EUTYCHIS ZOPYRION	servant (slave) to Praxinoa servant to Gorgo Praxinoa's baby boy

Praxinoa's house

GORGO   Are you at home, Praxinoa?

PRAXINOA
                                       Of course.
Dear Gorgo, what an age it's been! It's quite
Amazing that you made it here today. Get her a
chair, Eunoa. Find a cushion.

GORGO   Thank you, but I don't need one.

PRAXINOA
                                       Then sit down.

GORGO	I must be mad, my dear, from where I live
	I could hardly get here: such a crowd, so many
	Vehicles, the Household Cavalry, soldiers
	Everywhere. The road seemed endless, too.
	I never realized how far out you live.
PRAXINOA	My husband's off his trolley. He made us live
	In this disgusting place out in the sticks –
	It's not a home – so that we two could not
	Be neighbours. Spiteful beast, always the same!
GORGO	Hush, dear! Don't call your Dinon such bad names
	In front of the child. See how he stares at you.
	Zopyrion, it's all right: she doesn't mean
	Your daddy.
PRAXINOA	I'll swear the baby understands.
GORGO	Pretty daddy!
PRAXINOA	As for him, the other day –
	I said to him – it was just the other day –
	'Buy me those special bath salts, made with sea
	weed.'
	And all he brought was table-salt, he's so thick.
GORGO	And mine is just the same, my Diocleidas.
	Money runs through his hands. Five fleeces
	He bought me yesterday, seven drachmas' worth
	Of dog's hair, pieces pulled off an old bag,
	All rubbish: endless work to sort it out …
	Enough. Put your best gown on, and that coat
	With the nice brooch. We're going out to see
	The grand Adonis show at Ptolemy's palace.
	I've heard the Queen has put on something
	really Special.
PRAXINOA	And no expenses spared.
GORGO	We'll see it,
	Then boast of it to those who've missed it all.
	It's time to make a start.
PRAXINOA	Those who don't work
	Are always ready for a holiday.

They go out into the street

PRAXINOA   O heavens, what a crowd! How on earth do we
Get through this lot in time – it's like an ant-heap!
Yet, Ptolemy, since your father went to join
The immortal gods, you've made a difference.
No criminal assaults the passer-by,
No thief creeps up upon you secretly
In the old Egyptian style. They used to play
Their tricks on everybody, the lay-abouts.

My dear Gorgo! Look out! What shall we do?
The Guards are riding us down. Don't trample me!
That chestnut's rearing up. How wild it is!
Eunoa, don't flinch. It will destroy its rider.
Thank heaven I left the baby safe at home.

They arrive at the palace

GORGO   Praxinoa, look at that crowd in front of the gates.
PRAXINOA   Amazing. Gorgo, take my hand; Eunoa,
Hang on to Eutychis. Hold tight, or you'll
Get separated. All push in together!
Keep close to us, Eunoa. What a shame –
My summer coat is torn in half! Young man,
Will you please be careful: watch what you're
doing.
FIRST MAN   It's not my fault; we must all be careful.
PRAXINOA   What a crowd! It's like pigs at a trough.
MAN   Well done, ladies! We'll be there in good time.
PRAXINOA   Well, thank you, sir, for looking after us.
Such kindness from a man who took care of us.

Eunoa is crushed! Now, force your way! That's it!
'All in,' as the bridegroom said when he shut
the door.

Inside the palace

GORGO   Praxinoa, come this way. First, take a look at
The embroideries, so neat and delicate,
You'd say the garments were designed for the gods.

PRAXINOA	By Our Lady Athena! What kind of workers
	Laboured over them, what kind of artists
	Were able to draw such tiny little pictures?
	They are so real, they really seem to move:
	They are alive, and not just woven figures.
	A tribute to man's cleverness. Look at Him –
	The wondrous Boy lies on a silver couch,
	His downy beard just showing on His face.
	Three times Thou art beloved, our Adonis.
	Even in the Underworld Thou art beloved!
SECOND MAN	Keep quiet, you wretched females, mooing and
	cooing
	Like country pigeons – each vowel torn apart
	In your flat accents.
PRAXINOA	Where is this man from?
	What is it to you, if we speak in the Doric?
	Shout at your slaves in that rude way!
	Do you think
	You can order Syracusans about? What's more
	We are Corinthians, like Bellerophon.
	We speak the dialect of the Peloponnese.
	The Doric is allowed for Dorians,
	I trust . . .

Luckily this exchange is interrupted by the arrival of the singer. She sings a hymn which summons Aphrodite to weep for Adonis. The final ceremony will take place and Adonis will be sent out into the sea. The singer emphasizes the fact that he will return again every year in the spring-time, so illustrating a kind of immortality. The poem concludes with the two women agreeing to come to the festival again next year.

What is happening here? There is a series of scenes.

Answer

The women are living in a suburb and decide to go up to town, where they encounter the crowds of the city centre. Finally, they enter the palace which contains the shrine. The women give a description of the figures of Aphrodite and Adonis. The poem ends with a hymn.

Discussion

Adonis is very much the star of a women's festival, it seems. Notice the amusing dialogue. These women seem to be freer than their Athenian predecessors and have money to spend. Although the poem does not treat the religious element seriously, Adonis reawakens from death and dies again each year. This used to be interpreted as a 'vegetation-myth', and the Greeks would have been used to the return of Persephone each spring. The fact that Adonis had, in some sense, conquered death made him especially important to those who were looking for personal salvation.

Serapis

The Egyptians had worshipped Apis, who was incarnated as a bull. Since time immemorial the dead bulls had been mummified and kept in a subterranean repository. Osiris was the husband of Isis who was resurrected. Now the two cults were combined under the official sponsorship of the first Ptolemaic kings. A new god – Osiris-Apis – had been created. The construction of Serapis or Sarapis as a new composite deity was amazingly successful and later spread through the Roman Empire.

10 THINGS TO REMEMBER

1 In the fourth century BCE the Greek city-states were too weak to resist Philip of Macedon.

2 Alexander (336–323 BCE) conquered Egypt and the Persian Empire.

3 Alexandria was the name of several new cities founded by Alexander. Alexandria in Egypt became a world city.

4 Though the generals who succeeded Alexander split the empire, Greek culture spread through the entire area.

5 This marks the end of the Classical period. Artistic tastes changed, and larger and more florid buildings were constructed.

6 The new period of history is called Hellenistic, and lasted until Roman times.

7 Literature was encouraged by the foundation of the Library at Alexandria.

8 A new form of literature was the Pastoral, in which an idealized country life was represented.

9 Theocritus wrote many pastorals, but one of his works was a satirical poem about city life in Alexandria.

10 New forms of religious belief flourished. The cult of Adonis, who is reborn every year in the spring-time, shows the direction this movement was taking.

9

The legacy of Greek civilization – Byzantium

Aim

By the end of this chapter you should be able to understand how Greek culture survived through the Byzantine period and then down to the present day, appreciating at the same time that there are some problems of continuity.

At the end of this chapter you will have been introduced to one or two instances of the survival of Greek ideas and cultural symbols, and might begin to discuss them, realizing that fashion and the passage of time will not allow us to keep any consistent meaning in some of these icons. You may wish to debate whether the Elgin marbles should be returned from London to Greece.

The following are the important names introduced in this chapter together with their pronunciation.

BYZANTIUM (*bie-zan-tee-um*, though '*biz*' at the beginning is allowed; stress is on the second syllable). City lying on the straits between Europe and Asia, now Istanbul.

CONSTANTINE (*con-stan-tine* with stress on the first syllable). Roman emperor who re-founded Byzantium as an Imperial city that was called Constantinople.

HAGIA SOPHIA (*ah-yee-a sof-ee-a*). Means 'Holy Wisdom'; the huge domed church in Constantinople erected by the emperor Justinian in the sixth century CE.

Historical narrative

THE ROMAN EMPIRE

Most of Greece was absorbed by Rome during the second century BCE, and thereafter the Romans took over the remains of the Hellenistic kingdoms in what is now Turkey. From the time of Julius Caesar, Roman interest in Egypt eventually brought about the seizure of the last independent Greek-speaking area of any real power. When Antony and Cleopatra were defeated, the Hellenistic world ceased to exist.

THE RISE OF CHRISTIANITY

Though we are told that Christ spoke Aramaic, the Gospels were written in Greek and for this reason obtained a wide circulation. There is also a case to be made that the ideas at the beginning of St John's Gospel, which famously opens 'In the beginning was the Word', should be seen as an extension of the Greek philosophers' search for origins and first principles. You could say that in using the Greek language the Christians were making a bid to convert the known world. Most of the early Fathers of the Church were of Greek origin or Greek-speaking.

CONSTANTINE

From the time of Constantine, the first Christian emperor (272–337 CE), the balance of the Roman world was altered in two ways. When the state enfranchised the new religion, Greek regained its intellectual pre-eminence as the language of theological controversy; and the emperor founded a new imperial city in the Greek heartland which became the capital of the Roman world. Although this was officially known as Constantine's city, i.e. Constantinople, people continued to use its old name – Byzantium.

THE BYZANTINE EMPIRE

When the Roman Empire ended in the west, the eastern half continued to survive for 1,000 years. At one point in the sixth century, under Justinian, it reconquered much of the territory that had been lost in Africa and Italy. With the new strength of the Byzantine Empire the Greek language came back to political power as it were; it was also the language of the Orthodox Church. In the rich culture of the city many traditions were changed beyond recognition and there were times when the old pagan world and its gods seemed to have been forgotten. But, in fact, the work of scholarship continued and the texts of many authors have come down to us only through Byzantine sources.

Byzantine sites

ISTANBUL

This is, of course, the modern name for Constantinople. It was the largest city in Europe during the medieval period. We have records of Vikings, Arabs and others travelling immense distances in order to see something so amazing. The walls, which were finally breached in 1453 CE while the huge new cannon thundered and roared, are still visible today. The supreme achievement of Byzantine architecture is the dome of Hagia Sophia – the church of Divine Wisdom, built in 532–7 CE during the reign of Justinian. It is worth contemplating the contrast with the Parthenon, built 1,000 years previously, which was also – in a sense – dedicated to divine wisdom, that of Athena. Although it was turned into a mosque for many centuries, the church is now a museum.

Insight

Byzantine studies, which were a neglected area of scholarship, began to quicken in the early twentieth century. Many people will know of the two 'Byzantium' poems of W. B. Yeats, who also said:

I think if I could be given a month of Antiquity and leave to spend it where I chose, I would spend it in Byzantium, a little before Justinian opened St Sophia and closed the Academy of Plato ...

I think that in early Byzantium, maybe never before or since in recorded history, religious, aesthetic and practical life were one, that architect and artificers ... spoke to the multitude and the few alike.

A Vision

MISTRA (MYSTRAS)

If you have been on a tour of the Peloponnese you may have been disappointed with what remains of the famous city of Sparta. Nearby is the medieval town of Mistra; this replaced Sparta in the Byzantine period. A seemingly endless collection of walls and buildings straggle up a prominent hill and from the top you can look down on the plain of Lakonia. In climbing this hill you are tracing a journey through history, from the Classical period through to the last stages of the Byzantine Empire when Mistra was a centre of learning and scholarship. It was principally from here, as was noted in Chapter 1, that Greek manuscripts and ideas came to the West during the Renaissance.

Continuity

How have the Greeks survived, if their state disappeared in 1453 CE? Of course, there are some problems in establishing continuity between the Ancient Greeks and the present-day inhabitants of the Greek homeland.

▶ There were many invasions of the mainland Greek territory in the Middle Ages; from the sixth century CE peoples called the Avars (hence the town of Navarino, formerly Avarino), Vlachs from Wallachia, Slavs and Bulgars from the Balkans moved into Greece. However, the activities of Byzantine monarchs like Basil the Bulgar-slayer may have been a deterrent.

▶ After the year 1081 the Normans, Franks and later the Crusaders established principalities in the islands and the Morea (the new name for the Peloponnese) and were quickly followed by the Venetians and Genoese, who established trading posts.

▶ The advent of the Turks is best forgotten if you are speaking to a Greek; from the fourteenth century they slowly became the masters of much of the Balkans and Southern Europe.

▶ After the War of Greek Independence (1821–9), the country was slowly liberated from the Turks, but it took many years to acquire the present extent of territory. In the 1920s there was wholesale displacement of the Greek population from Istanbul and Asia Minor (Turkey) and the refugees had to be resettled, mainly in the area of Athens.

WHO ARE THE MODERN GREEKS?

I'm afraid this question conceals more than its apparent simplicity reveals. Modern Greeks believe that they are in all respects the descendants and heirs of the Ancient Greeks. Questions of national identity are involved.

Because of the political changes listed above some people used to think that the descendants of the Ancient Greeks had 'disappeared', except on remote islands. As was pointed out in Chapter 1, nowadays we are more sceptical about 'invasion' theories and more inclined to believe that, give or take a few well-documented displacements, most people have continued to live in the same places until the industrial and transport revolutions of the nineteenth and twentieth centuries. What is more important is the survival of the language.

THE CONTINUITY OF THE GREEK LANGUAGE

A language as subtle as this was an irreplaceable tool and was never lost. Modern Greek is still recognizably the same language, nearer in many ways to that of ancient times than Chaucer's English is to our own. There was, for a time, considerable debate about the need to use a form of language that resembled the ancient tongue, but the language that people actually speak – referred to as demotic Greek – is what you need to learn if you go to Greece today.

The legacy of Greek civilization in the modern world

THE SURVIVAL OF GREEK CULTURE AND IMAGERY

Rather than talk in a general way about the influence of Greek ideas, which is almost impossible to assess, I propose to look briefly at one or two tangible examples.

THE ELGIN MARBLES

If you visit the British Museum in London you will find tourists swarming around the sculptures that Lord Elgin removed from the Parthenon in the early nineteenth century (see the section on the Parthenon in Chapter 6). There is no doubt that these figures are now part of British culture (see Keats's sonnets, for example) and were used for training art students. In many other museums Greek sculpture was represented by plaster casts that served the same purpose.

Nowadays a form of resin could be used to make exact and more durable copies. Therefore, there is little point in exhibiting the originals which could be returned to Greece.

It is often said that the sculptures were purchased quite legally, according to the rules of the time, but the Greeks would answer that the Turks were in no position to sell the sculptures, anyway. Another argument is about the pollution generated by modern cities. The stonework of the temples in Athens is beginning to deteriorate because of this and it is said that the British are performing a service to the world in keeping the Parthenon sculptures in a museum environment in London. I leave it to you to decide what should happen to the Elgin marbles.

THE GREEK REVIVAL

What are the statues in Figure 9.1 called? Where in this book have you seen statues like this before? Where are these figures situated?

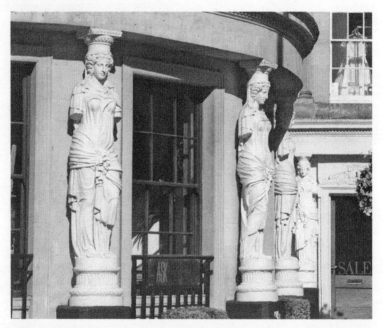

Figure 9.1 A mystery picture. In which town can you see these?

Answer

The figures are caryatids. You saw such figures – or replicas of them – on the porch of the Erechtheum in Athens. The figures in the picture and others like them are on buildings along the Promenade and in Montpellier Walk at Cheltenham in England.

Discussion

In some ways these statues are more perfect than they should be.
(You can compare them with one of the real caryatids which has
found its way into the British Museum.) Obviously this is because
they date from the Greek revival of the nineteenth century. You can
find such imagery elsewhere in imitations and reconstructions of
Greek buildings in many cities of the world. Why is Glasgow now
interested in preserving the buildings of 'Greek Thomson' – i.e.
Alexander Thomson (1817–75)? Why is Edinburgh called the Athens
of the North? Not just for its intellectual pre-eminence in the late
eighteenth century but because of the Classical buildings in the New
Town and elsewhere.

10 THINGS TO REMEMBER

1 After the second century BCE the Hellenistic states of the Mediterranean area were taken over by the Romans.

2 The Gospels were written in Greek, and speakers of the Greek language spread Christianity round the Eastern Mediterranean.

3 On the site of ancient Byzantium Constantine founded a new city called Constantinople. This is now known as Istanbul.

4 From that time the Eastern half of the Roman Empire is usually referred to as the Byzantine Empire.

5 The Byzantine Empire survived until 1453 CE, when the Ottoman Turks stormed the city of Constantinople.

6 Many scholars fled to Western Europe and increased the knowledge of the Greek language and the Classical texts.

7 Modern Greek is directly descended from the ancient language.

8 The arrival of the Elgin marbles in London encouraged Greek studies in literature and art.

9 In the nineteenth century there was a Greek revival in architecture.

10 There is now a debate – should the Elgin marbles be returned to Greece?

10

Taking it further

Tying everything together

In this final chapter a number of ways forward are suggested. These involve thinking about what we have done, visiting museums, reading more texts, or investigating special subjects through the latest modern introductions. Sometimes these activities blend together.

Cross-chronological thinking

There are a number of points that we need to go over again and expand because they do not easily lend themselves to the historical structure of the previous eight chapters. It is also relatively easy at this stage in the book to ask a number of general questions that sometimes get lost in the detail of dealing with a particular age. At any rate, some new ideas might be generated by redirecting the discussion to take in a wider angle. We have traced the civilization of the Greeks for approximately 2,000 years from the Mycenaeans to the fall of Constantinople, which is an amazingly long time. I suppose you might want to say that in the later stages it wasn't truly 'Greek' because it lost out politically to Alexander, the Romans and the Turks, but let's keep those suggestions to one side for the moment.

Why was Greek civilization so successful? You should concentrate on Athens in your answer.

Discussion

Remember that it is a civilization of individual cities. We need to start with Athens. A negative view might be that the city was always overstretched, too obsessed with ships and trade to sort out its land defences, its streets were thronged with foreigners, everybody seems to be pushing different ideas because of the democracy.

But all these things are its strength when turned around. You might have said that it was just like any large modern city that you know. (A book about London in the early nineteenth century called it 'the first world city', but there is a case for arguing that Athens aspired to become the Greek world city.) The apparent faults were what brought it to life, and explain why, above all, it was so full of ideas.

Sparta, on the other hand, was apparently more successful in the way that Thrasymachus tried to show in his analysis of society. It won the Peloponnesian War after all. Here might was right. But what have we got to show as evidence of Spartan culture and ideas? A few poems from the early period before the city was transformed. Then a succession of battle-honours, of conquests, of examples of bravery like that of Leonidas. Otherwise, like all the boring military dictatorships of our own time, it was dedicated to shutting down ideas and trying to preserve the status quo. (You might object here that, when it comes to shutting down ideas, the really bad thing about Athens that everybody remembers was the trial and death of Socrates, but though the issue is complicated this was after a defeat by the Spartans when the whole direction of the city had been temporarily thrown off course.)

In the later stages of Greek history Alexandria and Constantinople also qualify as world cities, both founded by god-kings, and not natural growths. The founders had learnt to place their cities between the East and the West; the rulers of Alexandria invested in the deliberate accumulation of knowledge, a kind of frightening parody of the picture we painted of Athens as the centre of ideas.

Constantinople was at first the centre of a kind of kingdom of God on earth. But the Greek passion for definitions led to theological controversies which we have difficulty in interesting ourselves in but which gave it life; this led on into amazing architectural developments that looked towards the future, even though the streets became a kind of 'Postmodern' museum of earlier Greek sculpture. One always forgets, in the usual concentration on Western Europe, points that were made in Chapter 9 – that Constantinople was the largest European city throughout the Middle Ages, and succeeded in holding together its empire for an amazing period of 1,000 years.

How did Greek civilization work – as a system?

Discussion

Look again at the map showing the trade routes (Figure 1.5). This
illustrates economic success. The whole structure of the colonies
worked to help imports – it safeguarded the grain route from the
Black Sea – and also to distribute exports. See how the oil and the
vases, for example, are transferred to the west, so that the best vases
turn up in places like Etruria. Cities like Athens and Corinth (Sparta's
ally) are positioned at the centre of this web, and this must be the
basis of their prosperity since they had few natural resources. Corinth
was particularly fortunate in its placing on the Isthmus because
it could trade easily to east and west; though the Corinth canal is
a recent construction the Greeks were able to move some of their
smaller vessels overland.

Ships and shipwrecks

It is therefore obvious that one of the clues to the success of the
system lay in the development of shipping. Far back in pre-history,
primitive boats were necessary to link up the scattered islands
of the Aegean Sea. As soon as really sea-worthy ships had been
developed, the systematic knitting together of the Mediterranean
world became possible. Some idea of the kinds of vessel that
were in use and their capabilities has always been known from
literature, for example, Homer's *Odyssey* and the tale of the
Argonauts are all about early seafaring. The archaeological site of
Akrotiri, at Santorini (Thera), has yielded pictorial evidence from
this early period, and the frescoes from this island are now to be
seen in the National Archaeological Museum in Athens. These
show surprisingly large galleys and sailing-vessels, though their
size may be exaggerated if this picture is fanciful rather than literal
in its depictions. Later representations of Greek ships may be
found on vases; in addition to ships with a square sail, presumably
used for trading, there are galleys with several banks of oars –
a bireme has two and a trireme three. The heavier vessels are
constructed with a ram for use in time of war. With these vessels
ancient technology had reached its limit, and they continued in use
throughout the Classical period.

The contribution of marine archaeology

In recent years it has been possible to explore the sea-bed in search of wrecks, and by the use of sounding devices a large number of these have been located, though only a few have yet been properly excavated. A merchant ship that sank near Kas in southern Turkey in about 1415 BCE has been assumed to be Mycenaean because of the evidence of weapons and pottery; of course these may have been acquired by trading. Because of the nature of the cargo it carried the ship may have come from the eastern Mediterranean. Although it was only about 17 metres long, it had a surprisingly rich cargo, including storage jars, some of which contained resins, and ingots of copper. Small items of jewellery, which help to date the wreck, may have belonged to the crew. Another vessel from the same area but a slightly later period contains bronze ingots and scrap metal. Thereafter the wrecks so far discovered are less exciting, being commercial vessels limited to one kind of cargo. Some quite strong vessels were used for heavier cargoes such as marble.

How did the Greeks defend their cities and empires?

A good question because we naturally prefer people to behave peacefully and are usually biased against militarism. (Notice how children study the *Roman* Army at school.) All the stages of Greek civilization are supported by conscious effort to keep up with or to advance the techniques of winning battles. Although the Mycenaean warriors used chariots and horses like most Bronze Age societies, the tactics which governed their deployment were forgotten during the Dark Ages, so that Homer, writing in c. 800 BCE, cannot understand their use in warfare; he sees them simply as taxis that deliver the heroes into the heart of the fighting. Homeric battles are strictly a matter for foot-soldiers; but at the end of the battle the heroes are whisked away by their chariots. In the Archaic and Classical Greek world the heavily armed soldier or hoplite dominated the fighting; such well-trained and disciplined troops accompanied Leonidas at Thermopylae. They were able to act together in formation (the phalanx), and must have been as formidable as a tank in obliterating the opposition. Sparta was defeated in the fourth century by Epaminondas of Thebes because he had invented a heavier phalanx and new manoeuvres for his soldiers. The Spartans had not learned to keep up with such developments, and later Alexander showed how cavalry could be used to secure astonishing victories. After this the military skill of the Romans dominated the scene, but it is worth remembering that the Byzantines held out against the barbarians and the Turks for so long because of their well-constructed defensive walls and their secret weapons, like 'Greek fire'.

Everyday life

A CHANGE OF EMPHASIS

In the eighteenth and nineteenth centuries, when the main interests of scholars were the political developments and the greater artistic monuments, the life of the people was largely ignored. The balance has been corrected in the twentieth century, and one of the pleasures of life is going round a museum, or looking at photographs of objects in a book, and remarking, 'But that is just the same as today!' I remember, while visiting a site in Euboea, being deceived in this way. Across the upper level of the dig ran a series of joined-up pipes, each approximately 2 metres long. 'Oh,' I thought, 'they have had to avoid disturbing that modern sewage system,' but was then informed that what I was staring at was a Hellenistic drain.

In the same way you can often see mason's and carpenter's tools, or agricultural implements such as hoes and spades, even from the Bronze Age, which closely resemble today's equivalents. Because they were often cast or moulded, some of these everyday objects even seem to be standardized factory-made products, which you could buy today at an ironmonger's or garden centre, though they will rarely look brand new. Pottery, too, encourages these thoughts; on the one hand there are 'one-offs', specially made vases for festivals or the winners of competitions, often specially ordered, and aspiring to be taken as works of art. But, on the other hand, there are thousands of storage jars, all of standard sizes and with the handles in the same place, which are as common and as useful as modern flowerpots or kitchen ware.

But where are the people who used them?

GRAVESTONES

Not only are the people dead and gone but the things on which they might have impressed their identity – their houses and furniture – have largely disappeared. The only exception is Akrotiri on Thera, already mentioned because of its frescoes, which was buried by a volcanic eruption and is the Pompeii of the early Greek world.

In Classical times only the gravestones or *stelai* (stone slabs) of ordinary people have survived. In the fifth century these have a pilaster (a column in relief) on each side, and a pediment at the top. The centre provides a picture of the dead person, but not what we could call a portrait. A father may be shown saying goodbye to his son. A woman is often accompanied by her baby, or children, and a maidservant. The men are sometimes seen at their occupation, making shoes, for example, or the tools of their trade can be displayed without a picture of the person at all.

Because there was no clear belief in an afterlife we can assume that these people are shown as they were, not as they are going to be. In spite of the fact that they were probably turned out in quantity, and may seem to show typical rather than individual pictures of human life, these grave-slabs are often more moving, incidentally, than more famous sculptures.

PICTURES ON VASES

Like most people, you probably tend to walk past the rows of vases on display in your local museum. You will find, if you persevere, that a lot can be found out by carefully examining the vases, even though the official description says that what you are looking at is a scene from mythology. You may see Circe at her loom, or Odysseus on his ship, without realizing that the model can only be the looms and ships of the artists' own time, since it is unlikely that they could have had any knowledge of how these things looked in previous epochs.

PERSONAL OBJECTS

Look out for the smaller things in the museum cases for an insight into people's lives and their personal tastes. Some of the jewellery will have been reassembled, but other pieces are intact. Because they were often dropped by their owners and then lost they were preserved in the earth largely undamaged. So you can find rings, sometimes with seals attached to make impressions, which may be too small to see, and are presumably in reverse. Here a magnifying device, or an enlarged photograph of the positive image alongside, will enable you to enter another world. Coins, too, although less personal in their origins, sometimes have tiny scenes depicted on them, or show something connected with their city.

Further study of authors and texts

Because this has not been a literature course, a number of important authors have been disregarded to keep the approach to the different stages of Greek civilization in proportion. Here I want to introduce you to some examples of texts with a more literary interest and emphasis.

TRANSLATIONS

Generally speaking, you will find what you want in the Penguin Classics series, which is so well established as to need no introduction. Indeed, some of the famous early translations, for example, E.V. Rieu *The Odyssey*, Penguin, 1945 have now been revised. For translations of less well-known authors than those chosen by Penguin, see the Loeb editions, where the Greek text is on the left-hand page. Originally the authors of the Penguin and other modern translations insisted on using prose to convey the meaning of the text exactly. Nowadays, there is much discussion of the inadequacy of prose translations to convey the feeling of a poetic text. Unfortunately, the resulting English poetry may either be stilted 'translationese' or a complex piece of modern poetry which may be dense and impenetrable.

HOMER

Of course you have met some sections of Homer in the early chapters but they were really being used to support the archaeology, and were therefore in a prose translation. If you would like to get the feel of Homer's verse, try the versions by Richmond Lattimore, who endeavoured to reproduce the lucidity of his author, and did not worry about using the same repetitions as the original:

The Iliad of Homer: translated with an introduction by Richmond Lattimore, University of Chicago Press, 1951.

The Odyssey of Homer: A modern translation by Richmond Lattimore, Harper and Row, New York, 1965.

Although it is often quite clear what Homer is saying, you will feel the need to explore the background to the text. It is possible to purchase commentaries that have the same line-numbers as these translations, and are extremely useful:

Malcolm M. Willcock, *A Companion to the Iliad*, based on the translation by Richmond Lattimore, University of Chicago Press, 1976.

Peter Jones, *Homer's Odyssey*, A Companion to the English Translation of Richmond Lattimore, Bristol Classical Press, 1988.

A prize-winning children's book with a compendious collection of images of relevant archaeological material is also highly recommended to bring the background to Homer to life:

Peter Connolly, *The Legend of Odysseus*, Oxford University Press 1986, paperback 1988.

Insight

Besides translations of Homer, two recent poets have tried to capture the essence of Homer's *Iliad* at a shorter length: see, for example, several volumes by Christopher Logue: *Kings*, 1991, *The Husbands*, 1994. These are collected together in *War Music*, Faber and Faber, 2000.

Alice Oswald, *Memorial*, Faber, 2011, is a more drastic reshaping, in which the *Iliad* is reduced by 4/5ths and is laid out like a Great War memorial. The book-jacket has a blurb that says:

'The resulting poem is a war memorial, written, as David Jones said, "in memory of all common and hidden men", and a profoundly responsive work which gives new voice to Homer's level-voiced version of the world.'

DRAMA

Besides the translations of Greek plays available in the Penguin Classics series, please note that a complete translation of tragic drama was produced in the 1950s:

D. Grene and R. Lattimore, *The Complete Greek Tragedies*, Chicago, 1959.

COMEDY

Comedy has not been discussed in the present book, but is worth looking into for two reasons. One is to understand how contemporaries reacted to current political events and characters – this is the function of the Old Comedy, which is represented by Aristophanes. They also contain scenes of low life, in contrast to the mythical world of tragedy;

the characters must also be speaking in a way that approximates to the received language and conversation of ordinary people.

Aristophanes' plays, which are available in Penguin editions, were written in the later fifth century at the time of the Peloponnesian War. Besides being obscene – in an open way that some have compared to pantomime or music hall – they contain delightful fantasy. *The Birds* is about two characters who wish to escape from Athens and found a new city in the sky. To do this they have to come to terms with the Birds who are dressed in the appropriate manner of each species; in fact, the appearance of the chorus of birds must have been a major and expensive feature of these productions. Occasionally, as here when the Birds address the audience, the play is lifted above itself:

> *Ye Children of Man! whose life is a span,*
> *Protracted with sorrow from day to day,*
> *Naked and featherless, feeble and querulous,*
> *Sickly, calamitous creatures of clay!*
> *Attend to the words of the Sovereign Birds*
> *(Immortal, illustrious, lords of the air),*
> *Who survey from on high, with a merciful eye,*
> *Your struggles of misery, labour, and care.*

These verses are taken from the nineteenth-century translation by John Hookham Frere.

The Frogs displays a similar pair of characters in the first scene, who are desperately seeking something. This time our heroes are the god Dionysus and his slave. (Remember that the theatre at Athens was named after Dionysus who was the patron of the main dramatic festival.) Sophocles and Euripides have just died, so Dionysus wishes to visit the house of Hades to bring back a dead poet to enliven the drama. Their journey leads them to a lake which it is necessary to cross over to reach the land of the dead. Dionysus, but not his slave, is allowed to embark with the help of the ferryman Charon, who then turns upon him.

CHARON: Hallo! What are you doing?

Dionysus is sitting idly at the side of the boat

DIONYSUS: What you told me to.
                I'm sitting at the oar.

CHARON: Sit over there,
                You horrible Fat Man. That's the place.

DIONYSUS: All right.
CHARON: Now move your hands and arms.
DIONYSUS: [*makes idiotic actions*]   Is that all right?
CHARON: You'd better stop all that. Pick up the oar,
              And pull away.
DIONYSUS: But how on earth can I?
              I've never served at sea, I'm just a land-lubber;
              I couldn't possibly do it...
CHARON: Yes, we can make you.
              As soon as you begin you'll hear some music
              That will teach you to keep time.
DIONYSUS: What music's that ?
CHARON: The Frogs in chorus – special singing Frogs.
DIONYSUS: Give me the time then.
CHARON: IN: and then pull OUT. IN: OUT.

They pass through a lake of Frogs who sing as Chorus the
noises which frogs actually make in Greece.

CHORUS   Brékeke -kéx ko-áx ko-áx
              brékeke -kéx ko-áx ko-áx
          children of the lakes and streams
              sing out your song
              let hymns ring out
              to our Lord Dionysus
                  ko-áx koáx
              the sweet refrain
              the ancient song
              to Nysa's lord
              the child of Zeus
          now calling together the folk of the fens
          to come to Our Town in the Marsh
          and shout aloud at the festival
                  Pot-Fair !
          Brékeke-kéx ko-áx ko-áx.
DIONYSUS: [*too slowly, stroke fading*]
              And I   begin   to feel   a pain
              My blistered bottom takes   the strain
                  Ko áx   Ko áx
CHORUS: [*increases the pace*]
              Brékeke-kéx ko-áx ko-áx

140

Eventually they reach Hades and a debate takes place about the merits of the poets. Euripides, who was supposed to be the choice of Dionysus, is pitted against Aeschylus in a series of contests that are more like games. Finally, a verse from each poet is weighed against a verse from the other on the balance. It is Aeschylus who is chosen to return to earth.

This play is more frequently revived than others and there have been several performances in swimming pools, with the Frogs swimming in formation.

LYRIC POETRY

This is almost impossible to translate fairly and is largely unconcerned with history. Homer's work has come down to us accompanied with long hymns to the gods. In the Archaic and early Classical periods especially on the Greek islands, we encounter very short lyrical poems, which seem to fulfil the Romantic ideals of our nineteenth century, when they were popular. In fact, it is difficult to translate the work of Archilochus, Alcaeus and Sappho without falling into Romantic phraseology.

SAPPHO

Here are two short poems, possibly fragments, of Sappho, in a literal translation.

> *The moon has set*
> *And the Pleiades*
> *It is the middle of the night*
> *Time passes*
> *And I lie alone.*

The second poem is about the evening star:

> *Hesper, you bring home all the things*
> *that the dawn dispersed in its light;*
> *you bring the sheep, you bring the goats,*
> *you bring the children back to their mother.*

PROSE

There is a wide variety of prose-writing, some of which we have already sampled. Here is an example of the writing of the historian Plutarch, whose parallel lives were used by Shakespeare as source material for his classical plays. Plutarch lived from about 50 CE to 120 CE.

Among his immense output is a dialogue *On the Decay of Oracles,* which contains stories about Britain. Some of them seem very odd, considering that it was now part of the Roman Empire and presumably explored.

> **Demetrios told us that there were a number of uninhabited islands around the coasts of Britain, and some of them are given the names of demons [i.e. spirits] and heroes. He said that he was sent by the Emperor to find out about these and to explore them, and landed on the island which lay next to the uninhabited ones; this had some people living on it, who were regarded as holy and were not troubled by the British. At the time of his arrival a great storm had just occurred with a lot of thunder and lightning in the air; a gale passed over and the stormwinds raged. When the weather became calm, the islanders told him he had witnessed the end of one of the great rulers of the world. They said that in the same way that a lamp does no harm when it is alight, but can annoy people no end when you put it out, so these great spirits are friendly and harmless when they burn brightly; but when they die and their light goes out, they generate high winds and tempests like the one he had experienced. They can sometimes infect the air with diseases.**
>
> **There is one island in that place where Kronos lies asleep; his prison is guarded by Briareus. It is sleep that holds him in chains, and many demons lie around him as his servants and followers.**

What do you make of this?

Discussion

It is certainly very odd. The writer is interested in demons (both a positive and negative idea like the djinns who inhabit lamps in Arabian stories). Although the time is now after the origins of Christianity Plutarch is not influenced by this, and seems in a strange way to be pursuing the same inquiring interests that we noted in Herodotus centuries before.

The resemblances to the stories of the Sleeping Beauty and to the 'Celtic' story of the Bondage of Merlin, who was bewitched into an eternal sleep, are very curious indeed. There has been some debate as to whether the Scilly Islands are referred to, or the Scottish islands beyond Mull which Demetrios is supposed to have visited.

Annotated booklist

There are plenty of books about the Greeks, but in general I am recommending only one or two in each section of this bibliography, because the next thing I think you should do is to get down to exploring a particular theme, building or literary work in detail. In working at a case-study or in simply following up an interest that you have already, you will pick up far more expertise yourself.

A good example of this way of working is provided by:

Mary Beard and John Henderson *Classics: A Very Short Introduction*, Oxford, 1995, reissued 2000. It is available as an e-book and an audio book.

The aim of this book is to show how the study of the Classics has been transformed into a very modern discipline. Using one main example – the temple of Apollo at Bassae – the authors take us from the British Museum, where its frieze is displayed, to Greece and then to the travellers who noticed and explored the site. This leads to examples of scholarly interpretation. This is a very exciting tour de force, stimulating further exploration.

GENERAL ILLUSTRATED HISTORY

John Boardman, Jasper Griffin and Oswyn Murray, eds. *The Oxford History of the Classical World*, Oxford University Press, 1986.

The three editors have put together a copiously illustrated and very readable collection of essays that cover the whole Greek and Roman period. It is a big book to handle and has now been split up in the paperback editions. You will need to consult the first Greek section for reference purposes but the whole work is a good read, especially if you want to find out what happens next in the Hellenistic and Roman periods.

PICTURE-BOOKS AND INTRODUCTIONS TO ARTISTIC THEMES

You will need to find well-illustrated books to explore Greek Art.

First there is a general up-to-date history of Classical Art in the same format as the book described first:

John Boardman, ed. *The Oxford History of Classical Art*, Oxford University Press, 1993.

(The same author has written on a number of areas of Greek Art, in particular useful hand-books on sculpture and vase-painting.) But you may find this book is too technical at times and will want to read something that helps you with a specific area.

BRITISH MUSEUM PUBLICATIONS

The British Museum produces a number of publications with good coloured illustrations; the examples are usually – but not always – drawn from its own collections. This can be helpful if you are using that museum, but as in all museums, not everything that the museum possesses can be kept on show. Examples are:

Jenifer Neils, *Concise Introduction to Ancient Greece*, British Museum Press, London, 2008.

Dyfri Williams, *Greek Vases*, British Museum Press, London, 1985, reprinted 1995. This has helpful discussions of clay, firing and technique.

J. Lesley Fitton, *Cycladic Art*, British Museum Publications, 1989.

B.F. Cook, *The Elgin Marbles*, British Museum Press, 1984, Second edition 1997. This contains a history of the Parthenon, and explains clearly how the marble sculptures were arranged as part of the original building; it reproduces some early drawings and prints to illustrate this. Its main subject is Lord Elgin's expedition and, of course, the arrival of the marbles in London and the various ways in which they have been displayed since that time.

And see Ian Jenkins, *The Parthenon Sculptures in the British Museum*, British Museum Publications, London, 2007

SCULPTURE

The most attractive introduction at the time of writing is probably:

Nigel Spivey, *Understanding Greek Sculpture: Ancient Meanings, Modern Readings*, Thames and Hudson, London, 1996.

This book accepts from the beginning that the surviving sculpture has been displayed in a variety of ways and explores the cultural history of these artworks and their meaning.

ARCHITECTURE

The following surveys are in the 'Classical Bookshelf' series:

R.A.Tomlinson, *Greek and Roman Architecture*, British Museum Press, London, 1995.

and for theatres and the physical remains of drama:

Richard Green and Eric Handley, *Images of the Greek Theatre*, British Museum Press, London, 1995.

Finally, Eyewitness Guides have produced a compendium of images designed for school use:

Anne Pearson, *Ancient Greece*, Dorling Kindersley, London, 1992.

GREEK PRE-HISTORY

A summary of the controversy about the distant origins of the Greeks, and the relation of Greek to other languages, is provided by:

Colin Renfrew, *Archaeology and Language: The Puzzle of Indo-European Origins*, Jonathan Cape, London, 1987.

For the Mycenaeans a picture book is useful; see

W.D.Taylour, *The Mycenaeans*, Thames and Hudson, London. 2nd edition revised 1990. Recent work is conveniently summarized in:

K.A. and Diana Wardle, *Cities of Legend: The Mycenaean World*, Classical World series, Bristol Classical Press, 1998.

MYTHOLOGY

There is a short introduction with useful illustrations:

Lucilla Burn, *Greek Myths*, British Museum Publications, London, 1990.

For reference purposes note that you can look up all the myths in:

P. Grimal, *The Dictionary of Classical Mythology*, Blackwell, Oxford, 1986. It also contains tables of the complicated genealogies and helpful lists at the back.

ATLAS

The most recent historical atlas with coloured maps and a number of useful supporting photographs is:

Robert Morkot, *The Penguin Historical Atlas of Ancient Greece*, Penguin Books, Harmondsworth, 1996.

GENERAL REFERENCE

A good library will have a classical dictionary where any topic can be followed up. The latest scholarly production, subtitled rather charmingly as 'The Ultimate Reference Work on the Classical World', is:

Simon Hornblower and Antony Spawforth eds., *The Oxford Classical Dictionary*, Oxford University Press, 4th edition, 2012.

HISTORY OF LITERATURE

The most generously appreciative history of Greek literature that is readily available is:

Peter Levi, *The Pelican History of Greek Literature*, Viking 1985 and Penguin Books, Harmondsworth,1985.

MODERN NOVELS AND SPECIAL STUDIES

Another way of approaching the Greek world is through historical novels. Unfortunately these soon date, not in their accuracy but in the period-flavour of their own times which they unconsciously transmit. Mary Renault is still much praised.

Mary Renault, *The Praise Singer*, John Murray, London 1978. Also available in Penguin Books, 1990. This is not just a good read; hiding behind the novel is a biographical study of Simonides the early Greek lyric poet. She has also produced a trilogy of novels about Alexander.

Among other more general books mentioned in the main body of this book was:

Edward W. Said, *Orientalism*, Routledge and Kegan Paul Ltd, London, 1978, Peregrine Books (Penguin), 2003. This endeavoured to explain the sources of the modern concept of orientalism by going back to Herodotus and the Greek view of foreigners. This is a particularly important book because it shows how Western civilization has internalized negative as well as positive Greek concepts and still employs them.

GUIDE-BOOKS TO GREECE

Even if you can't visit Greece it would be a good idea to look at some of these, though the choice for more literary works will depend on your own country and its travellers.

The most famous guide-book to Greece was written in Roman times by Pausanias. He was still able to see most of the monuments before they were destroyed or dispersed. The text is available in English – slightly rearranged – in:

Peter Levi (translator) *Pausanias: Guide to Greece Volume 1: Central Greece*, and *Volume 2: Southern Greece*, Penguin Classics, Harmondsworth, 1971 reprinted.

While it is amusing to consult this before visiting a site you will need a proper guide-book to take with you. The *Blue Guide*, now published by Somerset Books, London, is frequently updated and has always been the most useful complete companion to the history of the Greek cities and villages; for the archaeological sites it contains black and white diagrams supported by a thorough discussion of what can be seen.

Recently two guide-books have been issued in the Eyewitness Travel Guides, which are more pictorial in their approach and use colour throughout; these are:

Greece: Athens and the Mainland, Dorling Kindersley, 2011 and *The Greek Islands* in the same series.

THE GREEK REVIVAL

As has been mentioned, you may have been living next to examples of Greek Revival architecture from the eighteenth and nineteenth centuries, which are worth studying for their own sake as well as giving you insight into the structures on which they are modelled. Your local reference library will probably contain a local studies collection to help you. Some cities have produced specialist guides. A good example is: [Fiona Sinclair for the] City of Glasgow District Council Planning Department, *Alexander Greek Thomson: The Glasgow Buildings*, 1990. This contains maps and trails so that you can easily locate the buildings.

Visiting museums

It is surprising how much material is stored up in museums all round the world. If you go to Athens you will want to see the National Archaeological Museum, which has the gold of Mycenae, including 'the Mask of Agamemnon' which Schliemann claimed to have

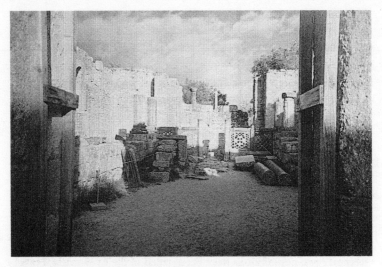

Figure 10.1 Olympia Today – Workshop of Pheidias

discovered. It also has the frescoes from the island of Thera (Santorini), which open a window on to Bronze Age life. Its main galleries also contain chronological displays of Archaic and Classical sculpture.

Other Greek sites we have mentioned, for example, Olympia, Delphi and Pylos, have their own museums. Some of these have recently been re-arranged and the material is much easier to understand.

In many cases you will need perseverance to get the best out of many famous museums in Britain and elsewhere. The material is often out of sight, except for the best-known objects. It has frequently been recovered from particular excavations and is therefore kept together; rarely is it possible to find everything displayed. There are special collections that are often kept together in drawers and cupboards. A large number of early purchases from the Turks – not just the Elgin marbles – have found their place in the British Museum. The Ashmolean Museum in Oxford has most of Sir Arthur Evans' Cretan discoveries. The Royal Scottish Museum in Edinburgh has a small collection of some of the best Greek vases in the world. The Burrell Collection in Glasgow shows how much could still be accumulated in quite recent times if you had enough money. It is now possible to find out the contents of many museums by using the internet.

NOTES ON THE BRITISH MUSEUM COLLECTIONS

Although *Teach Yourself* is an international series, in conclusion I should like to supply some more detailed notes on the British Museum collections as they are visited by students from all over the world, and illustrations are available in many books. (This is also an example of good practice; you will need to go to your local or nearest museum which contains Greek artefacts again and again in order to familiarize yourself fully with the culture of the ancient world.)

Since the rebuilding of the central section of the museum, you will find some objects in odd places: for example, there are a couple of lions from the Mausoleum on the main staircase. The collections of Greek objects are at present displayed in the following way.

If you turn left at the main entrance and go through the cloakroom, you will find in the next room (Gallery 6) that materials from the Treasury of Atreus at Mycenae are displayed around the door facing you and on the left. Go through this door into Gallery 11; this is a small room with a display of Cycladic figurines and early pottery from 1800–1550 BCE. The next, Gallery 12, is divided between two historical periods: 12a is devoted to the Minoans who lived in Bronze Age Crete; 12b is concerned with the Mycenaeans, and contains material from Mycenae and Troy. Notice on the left the coffins, which are so like reused bath tubs; and on the right you can see a Linear B tablet: it looks black. At the very end is a large krater (vase) showing a many-oared vessel and two figures; they are variously described as Paris and Helen, or Ariadne with either Theseus or Dionysus.

Turn right into Gallery 13, which contains Greek vases from 1050 to 520 BCE. Though these may seem intimidating in such a large quantity, it is worth trying to sort them out. You can see on your left the earliest pots; they are large vessels in the Geometric style. They have differently patterned bands of colour, but one or two of them show warriors with H-shaped shields, which may be from Homer's time or earlier. The central cases display Athenian 'black-figure' vases, and on them we can find familiar figures from the Trojan War, but the scenes are from other parts of the story than that narrated by Homer. On one amphora Achilles is fighting the Amazon Penthesileia. On another there is a scene from the end of the war: the Greek heroes are killing Polyxena, a Trojan princess, in order to secure a safe voyage home.

In the nearby case with material from Corinth you can see bronze helmets from 700–500 BCE. On the wall to your left are a few pieces from early Sparta; notice the small figures dedicated by children at the shrine of Artemis Orthia. Finally, on the far wall is some pottery from the eastern Greek cities. Look at the large plate showing Menelaos and Hektor fighting over the body of Euphorbos.

The small room, Gallery 14, explains the change from red vases with black figures to red figures on a black background. Gallery 15 has a bust of Pericles in the centre of the room, and another large collection of vases from the Classical period; to help you they have been arranged thematically. See the lettering shown at the top of each case. The first ones are:

▶ Democracy – with a scene of people voting.
▶ The human body – showing how it was becoming more naturalistic in its portrayal.
▶ The Persian Wars – notice the arrow heads from Marathon.
▶ People of Athens – there is a splendid storyteller, perhaps showing how Homer was recited.
▶ Empire – includes coins from Melos; and a vase showing Apollo and Artemis on the sacred island of Delos.

Architecture and sculpture now begin to dominate the displays. Gallery 16 has the frieze from the temple of Bassae, showing the battles between the Greeks and the Amazons, and the Lapiths and Centaurs. In Gallery 17 the Nereid monument from Lykia has been re-erected with its sculpture laid out alongside. Across to the left are the Elgin marbles in Gallery 18; watch the slideshows in the side room that show how the sculptures were arranged, and also how colour was applied. The main room attempts to reconstruct the shell of the Parthenon, so that you can understand how the frieze was arranged.

Go back to the monument in Gallery 17. Behind this you can go through into Gallery 19, which contains a Caryatid column from the Erechtheum, and the frieze from the temple of Athena Nike. There are also some fifth century grave slabs, which contrast with the official sculpture. Notice the cobbler.

The next rooms show later periods. Gallery 20 is from 400–325 BCE, and 21 is devoted to the Mausoleum of Halicarnassus, one of the wonders of the Ancient World. You can see from the scale of the figures that this was a huge monument. With Gallery 22 you encounter Alexander the Great and the Hellenistic period that followed his conquests; there is an interesting section on Egypt. Finally, Gallery 23 gives examples of Greek sculpture in the Roman period.

Upstairs there are the cases showing Greek and Roman life in gallery 69; these are not arranged in chronological order but by theme, for example, 'Writing' also contains a Linear B tablet, but a vase showing Odysseus and the Sirens is displayed under 'Ships and trade'. Further adjacent galleries show material from the Greek colonies in Cyprus and south Italy. Although it is possible to make an acquaintance with this material in one day, you should be prepared to return again and again, and study only a few objects at a time.

Websites

There are so many websites, especially for children and their homework, that you can try one and go further if you wish.

www.ancientgreece.com

Tourist sites are invaluable if you are unable to visit Greece, or simply looking for pictures. Try:

www.greeka.com/greece-archaeological-sites.htm

There is a fantastic website at:

www.greekmyth.org

This is not just about Greek myth; it opens lists of almost everything you could wish for. It provides links to university websites.

If you cannot visit the British Museum use 'Compass':

www.britishmuseum.org/compass

Here a large number of objects from the collections are displayed.

Index